Goodbye, Boys! Goodbye!

A Walking Guide to the

High Water Mark July 2–3, 1863

by

JoAnna M. McDonald

BSP Burd Street Press

This Burd Street Press publication
was printed by
Beidel Printing House, Inc.
63 West Burd Street
Shippensburg, PA 17257-0152 USA

In respect for the scholarship contained herein, the acid-free paper used in this book meets the guidelines for permanence and durability of the Committee on Production Guidelines for Book Longevity of the Council on Library Resources.

For a complete list of available publications
please write
Burd Street Press
Division of White Mane Publishing Company, Inc.
P.O. Box 152
Shippensburg, PA 17257-0152 USA

Library of Congress Cataloging-in-Publication Data

McDonald, JoAnna M., 1970-
Goodbye, boys! Goodbye! : a walking guide to the high water mark, July 2–3, 1863 / by JoAnna M. McDonald.
p. cm.
Includes bibliographical references and index.
ISBN 1-57249-104-3
1. Gettysburg (Pa.), Battle of, 1863. 2. Gettysburg National Military Park (Pa.)--Guidebooks. I. Title
E475.53.M427 1999
973.7'349--dc21 99-13311
CIP

PRINTED IN THE UNITED STATES OF AMERICA

Dedication

To the boys of '63

Requiescat In Pace

As the Confederate advance began toward Cemetery Ridge on July 3, the men called out to their comrades who were wounded during the cannonade,

"Goodbye, boys! Goodbye!"

Contents

Acknowledgments

I would like to thank my family, Mike Hardy, and many other friends who support me through the long and trying times of writing and researching my books.

Special thanks to Mr. Charles Hathaway, licensed Gettysburg tour guide. Mr. Hathaway acted as my fact editor and provided excellent suggestions for improving the manuscript. In addition to Mr. Hathaway, David Shultz, noted authority on Union artillery at Gettysburg, took the time to critique my maps.

As always, the staff and historians at the Military History Institute, in Carlisle, Pennsylvania showed great cooperation in this project. D. Scott Hartwig, head ranger at the Gettysburg National Park, and many other rangers at the park, should also be mentioned.

Introduction

Houses near and on Cemetery Ridge

Six houses stood near and on Cemetery Ridge during the battles on July 2–3 (see master map). William Bliss owned a farm about halfway between Seminary and Cemetery Ridge. At the time of the battle he had a huge barn and orchard. Confederate soldiers occupying the buildings were sniping at the Union troops on Cemetery Ridge. Consequently, on the morning of July 3, a detachment from the 12th New Jersey captured the barn, but were overwhelmed by numbers and forced to retreat. Four companies from the 14th Connecticut were then ordered to take the buildings. Heavy fighting occurred, and the 14th recaptured the barn. Yet, because the buildings were close to the Confederate line, the Union troops burned the farm buildings. The farm was never rebuilt. One can, however, see part of the Bliss orchard which is again growing.[1]

About one-fourth of a mile east of the Bliss farm, Abraham Bryan, a free black man, owned a 12-acre farm. (At least four other black families resided in the area.) Bryan lived in this house from 1857–1867. Some personal accounts inaccurately stated Major General George G. Meade, commander of the Army of the Potomac, used this house as his headquarters. Bryan's house was not Meade's headquarters. Possibly Union Brigadier General Alexander Hays commandeered Mr. Bryan's house as his division headquarters.[2]

On July 3 Mississippi and North Carolina troops reached the Bryan barn, and fought for a few minutes behind the structure. Union troops from New Jersey and New York were deployed in his yard.

Bryan also owned a small, one-story tenant house on the Emmitsburg Road. Another free black man, Alfred Palm, 25 years old, and Margaret Divit, a mulatto, lived in this modest dwelling. The house no longer stands.

A second neighbor of Bryan's was J. Worley Jones, also a black man. He, too, resided in a house on the Emmitsburg Road. Jones owned about four acres of land. The specific

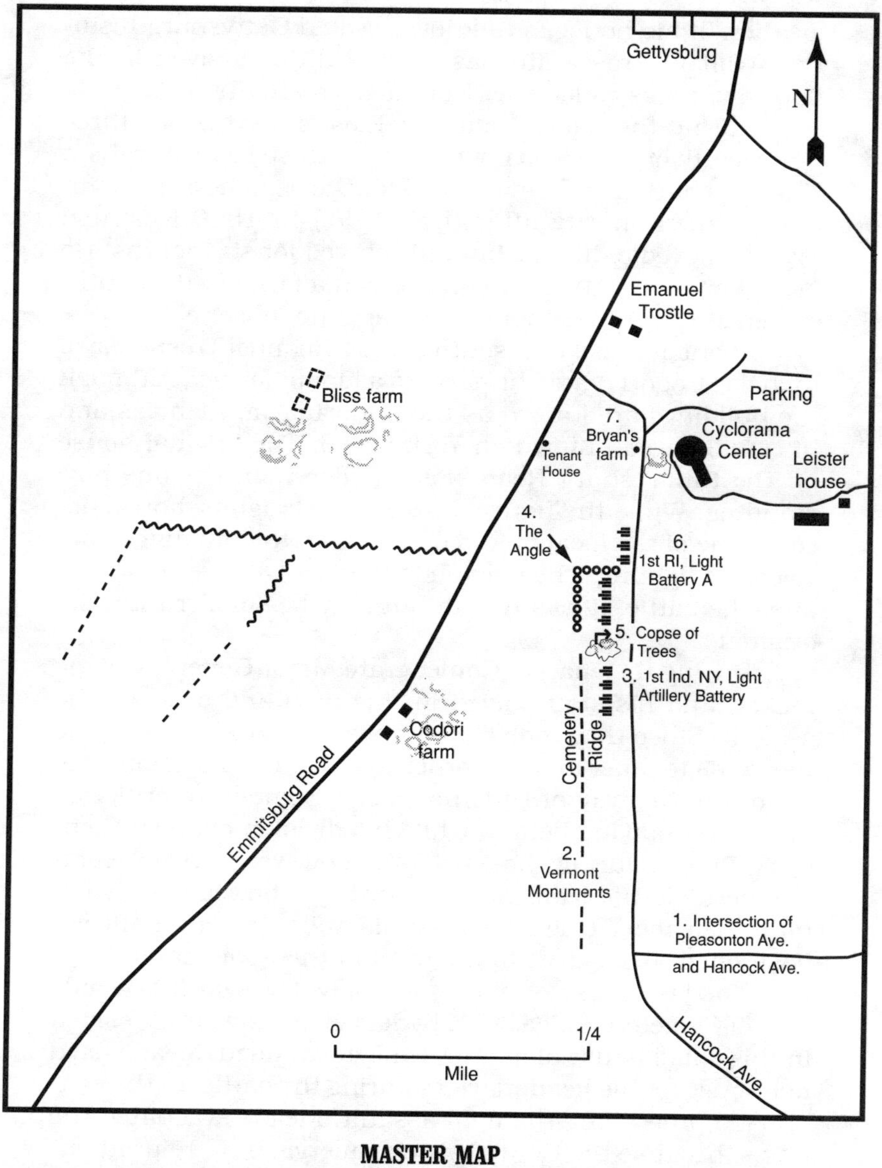

MASTER MAP

Stop 1: Intersection of Pleasonton and Hancock Avenues. **Stop 2:** Vermont Monuments **Stop 3:** Monument of 1st Independent New York Light Artillery Battery, Cowan's battery **Stop 4:** "The Angle." **Stop 5:** Copse of Trees. **Stop 6:** Cannon of 1st Rhode Island Ligh Artillery, Battery A. **Stop 7:** Bryan's farm.

location of his house is unknown. Noted Gettysburg historian William Frassanito has surmised Jones lived in the house which is called the "Emanuel Trostle" house.[3]

During the battle Emanuel Trostle lived about three miles south of town. (Do not get him confused with Abraham Trostle. Abraham's farm is noted for the dead horses photograph taken shortly after the battle.) In 1866 Emanuel Trostle moved to Illinois but only stayed for six months. He moved back to Gettysburg and rented a farm on the southern end of town. The house and farm no longer exist.[4]

About one-half mile south of the "Emanuel Trostle" farm Nicholas Codori rented his farm to a tenant farmer. Although the buildings are known as the Codori farm, Nicholas and his family lived in town on York Street. The original house on the Emmitsburg Road was smaller than the one now standing. While the house, barn, and slaughter house became one of the focal points of July 2–3, the buildings survived the fighting. The barn, however, caught fire sometime after the battle. It was rebuilt but may be smaller than the original.

During the charge, Confederate Major General George Pickett and his staff stayed in this area and oversaw the assault. Since they rode horses, it is reasonable to assume they rode to other areas in order to study the situation or to get out of the way of Union artillery. Some have criticized Pickett for staying behind while his division charged Cemetery Ridge. During the Civil War, however, division commanders did not lead their units; they followed closely behind their men. Brigadier generals and regimental officers positioned themselves to the front of their command.

The last house of note is actually one-eighth of a mile east of Cemetery Ridge. Mrs. Lydia Leister, a widow, resided in this small house along the Taneytown Road. Meade used her house for his headquarters during the battle. In the cannonade proceeding the final assault, Meade evacuated the house because the Confederate artillerymen were unintentionally overshooting Cemetery Ridge. Consequently, the Taneytown Road area was a very dangerous place.

All the buildings mentioned, except for Mr. Bliss' farm, were used as hospitals after the battle—as well as many other houses within the town and the outlying area.

Mr. Abraham Bryan's house

He was a free black man. His property became one of the focal points of Pettigrew's and Trimble's divisions.

USAMHI (United States Army Military History Institute)

Mrs. Lydia Leister's house and Major General Meade's headquarters.

The house and barn were terribly damaged during the cannonade.

USAMHI

Summary of Wednesday, July 1, 1863

The Battle of Gettysburg began on Wednesday, July 1, at around 7:00 a.m. Confederate General Robert E. Lee had ordered his corps commanders to rendezvous near the town. Yet, he did not expect to fight at this place. On the morning of July 1 a Confederate division, commanded by Major General Henry Heth, made a forced reconnaissance toward Gettysburg. They were, however, detained by Union Brigadier General John Buford's cavalrymen positioned on McPherson's Ridge, about one mile west of town. For three hours the dismounted horsemen checked the infantrymen. Finally, the Confederates made a forced assault and pushed the cavalrymen from their position. At this time (between 10:30–10:45 a.m.) Major General John Reynolds arrived at Gettysburg with two Union brigades. Recognizing the strong defensive position in and around the town, Reynolds determined to stand and fight there. Shortly after his arrival on the field, while directing the Iron Brigade into battle, he was shot and killed. For nine hours the two sides battled (7:00 a.m.–4:00 p.m.). By 4:00 p.m. the two Union corps (I and XI) were overwhelmed by sheer numbers. They retreated back through the town and established a strong defensive position on Culp's Hill, Cemetery Hill, and Cemetery Ridge. Exhausted and disorganized by the day's fighting, the Confederates broke off their attack.

Casualties:

The casualty list for July 1 was extremely high. The 26th North Carolina Regiment, that clashed primarily with the 24th Michigan, sustained the worst casualties. In about two hours' fighting the 800 North Carolinians engaged suffered 588 killed or wounded; 212 remained.

Overall Union soldiers killed and wounded on this day were at least 5,355. The Confederates lost 5,882 men, a total of 11,237 in only nine hours of fighting.[5]

*****

Lee and His Generals Take the Initiative
Evening of July 1 to Mid-Afternoon, July 2, 5:00 p.m.–3:00 p.m.

As the fighting subsided on July 1, Lee, and Lieutenant General James Longstreet, considered the situation. As the commander of the Confederate First Corps, Longstreet was Lee's chief lieutenant. Through field glasses they studied the Union position on Culp's Hill and Cemetery Hill/Ridge. Longstreet concluded that the Union line was too strong at that point, and he advised Lee not to attack at Gettysburg. Instead, he suggested that they make a sweeping movement southward along their own right, then veer toward the east to move around the left of Meade's army. Characteristically, Longstreet preferred to locate a strong defensive position and make the enemy come to him. Lee, however, stated that if the Union army remained in Gettysburg on July 2, he would attack.

Lee based his strategy on information that the Union line extended along Culp's Hill, Cemetery Hill, and stopped somewhere on Cemetery Ridge (where the Pennsylvania monument now stands). He proposed a three-pronged attack upon their position.

1) Longstreet was ordered to secretly position his troops on the right flank and command the main thrust of the attack. His men would attack up the Emmitsburg Road, roll up the Union left flank and hit their line on Cemetery Ridge/Hill.

2) Part of the Third Corps, commanded by Lieutenant General Ambrose P. Hill, would strike the Union center on Cemetery Ridge and Cemetery Hill and seek to prevent reinforcements from aiding either flank.

3) Lieutenant General Richard Ewell's corps, on the Confederate left flank, would make a "simultaneous demonstration upon the enemy's right [near Culp's Hill and east-Cemetery Hill] to be converted into a real attack should opportunity offer."[6]

Lee had approximately 55,000 troops and 268 cannon at his disposal.

*****

Meade Deploys the Union Army
Thursday, July 2, 1:00 a.m.–3:00 p.m.

The Army of the Potomac's commander, Major General George Gordon Meade, reached Gettysburg around 1:00 a.m. on July 2. Informed that Lee was concentrating his army around the town, Meade determined to stand and fight. Throughout the morning he reconnoitered the areas of

Cemetery Hill, Cemetery Ridge and Culp's Hill. As his army arrived piecemeal, Meade stationed troops on Culp's Hill, Cemetery Hill and Ridge. A strong defensive position was established for several reasons: 1) Two subordinate generals had expressed their disapproval of taking the offensive; 2) One corps still had not arrived; 3) Meade realized his men were worn out from intense marching and might not be able to sustain the strain of an offensive assault. 4) Lastly, he recognized the high ground as a natural defensive position and would provide them the advantage.[7] By 3:00 p.m. the entire Army of the Potomac was massed around Gettysburg. At least 75,000 soldiers and over 350 cannon were at Meade's disposal[8] and were deployed in strategic locations.

Stop 1

Intersection of Pleasonton and Hancock Avenues

General Robert Edward Lee, age 56
Commander of the Army of Northern Virginia. West Point graduate 1829, 2/46. Lee and Meade had served together in the Mexican War.

USAMHI

Major General George Gordon Meade, age 47
Received command of the Army of the Potomac three days before the battle. Graduated from West Point in 1835, 19/56.

USAMHI

Go to Intersection of Pleasonton Avenue and Hancock's Avenue. For convenience remain here for following narration of the second day's fighting on Cemetery Ridge.

The Battle for Cemetery Ridge

Thursday, July 2
Sometime after 6:00 p.m.

CONFEDERATE:

Third Corps
Lieutenant General Ambrose Hill

Brigade Commander
Perry's brigade (Lang)
Colonel David Lang

5th Fla., 8th Fla., 2d Fla.
742

Brigade Commander
Wright's brigade
Brigadier General A. R. Wright
1,413

3d Ga., 22d Ga., 48th Ga.,
2d Ga. battalion

UNION:

III Corps
Major General Daniel Sickles

and

II Corps
Major General Winfield Hancock

Brigade Commanders, III Corps*
First Brigade
Brigadier General Joseph Carr

1st Mass., 11th Mass., 16th Mass.,
12th N.H., 11th N.J., 26th Pa.

Second Brigade
Colonel William R. Brewster

70th N.Y., 71st N.Y., 72d N.Y.,
73d N.Y., 74th N.Y., 120th N.Y.

Brigade Commanders, II Corps
First Brigade
Brigadier General William Harrow
1,033

19th Maine,† 15th Mass., 82d N.Y.

Second Brigade
Brigadier General
Alexander S. Webb
1,224
69th Pa., 71st Pa., 72d Pa.,
106th Pa.

Third Brigade‡
Colonel Norman J. Hall,
922
19th Mass., 20th Mass., 7th Mich.,
(42d N.Y., 59th N.Y., four companies)

* No exact strength can be given for Carr and Brewster's brigades. Both units had suffered heavy casualties along the Emmitsburg Road.

† The 19th Maine primarily fought Lang's brigade.

‡ The 13th Vermont also battled against Wright's brigade. They belonged to the I Corps.

Due to confusion, Longstreet's attack did not begin until later in the day, around 4:00 p.m. Hill's men as well struck the Union line late, sometime after 6:00 p.m. In addition, Hill only sent in three brigades—Brigadier General Cadmus M. Wilcox's Alabama brigade, Colonel David Lang's Florida brigade, and Brigadier General Ambrose R. Wright's Georgia brigade. Even though Hill's attack did not coordinate with Longstreet's, his three brigades quickly swept the Union line on the Emmitsburg Road. A sizeable gap was now created in the Union line.

To help repulse these Confederate units Union Major General Winfield Hancock sent in three New York regiments and one Minnesota regiment. The New York regiments charged into Brigadier General William Barksdale's brigade (this unit belonged to Longstreet's First Corps). To the New Yorkers' right the 1st Minnesota, with only 262 men, struck Wilcox's brigade which numbered approximately 1,700. Colonel William Colvill, Jr., 1st Minnesota, fell, shot in the foot. Many other Minnesotans collapsed as well, wounded or killed. (The 1st Minnesota suffered 215 casualties out of 262; only 47 remained for active duty. On July 3, during Pickett's charge, they lost another twenty-four. Wilcox's brigade listed many casualties due in part to the annihilating artillery fire which they faced. Of their 1,700 men, they lost 577 killed and wounded.)

Colonel David Lang's Florida brigade, 700 men, advanced toward the position on which you are standing. The Union men which had been positioned on the Emmitsburg Road now faced about and attempted to regroup. With the help of Lieutenant Evan Thomas' six Napoleon guns, the realigned Union troops sent a volley into Lang's and Wilcox's brigade. The 19th Maine of Colonel Norman Hall's brigade then charged the Florida brigade. The 20th Massachusetts followed in support (see map 1). At nearly the same time Lang noted infantrymen to his right. (He probably saw the 1st Minnesota and the three New York regiments.) He, therefore, ordered his brigade back to the Emmitsburg Road, and then back to Spangler's Woods.[1] (During this engagement Colonel Paul J. Revere, grandson of the Revolutionary War hero, was struck by shell fragments in the chest; he died July 5.)

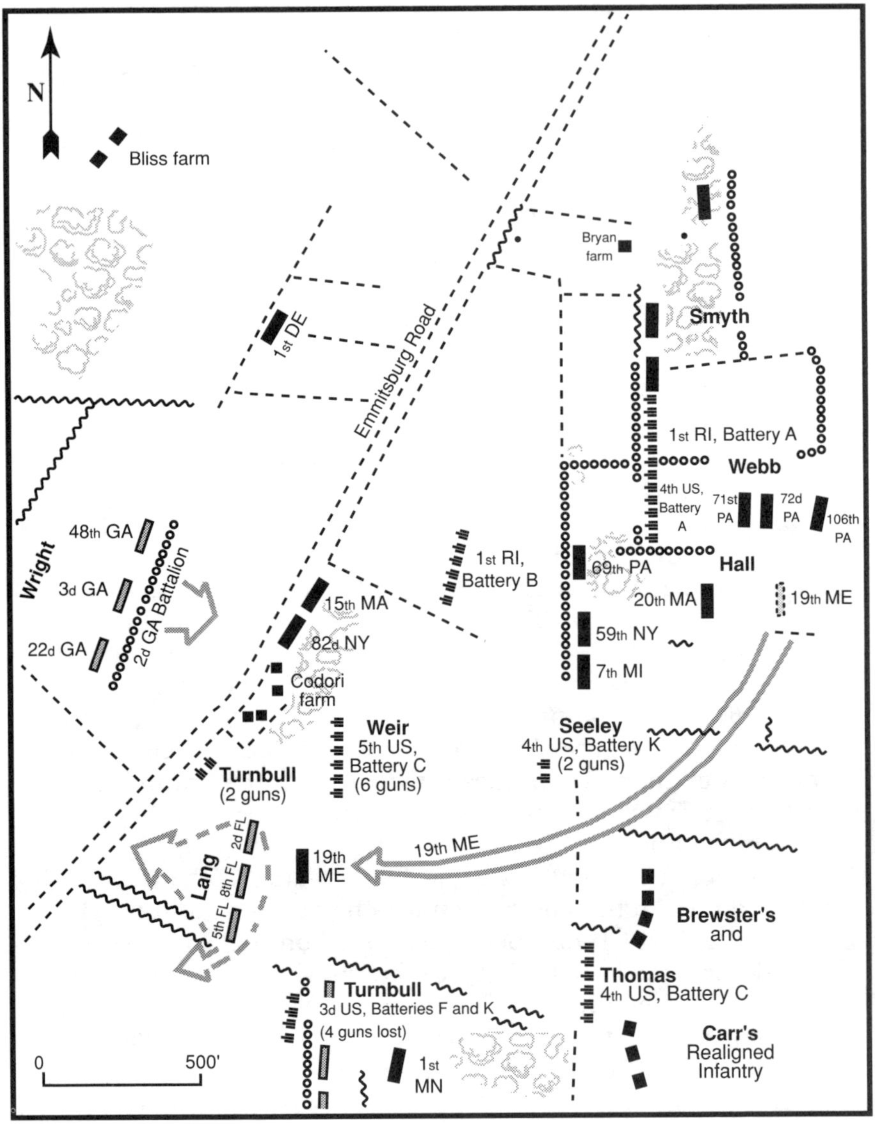

MAP 1

Stop 1: Intersection of Pleasonton and Hancock Avenues

July 2, sometime after 6:00 p.m.

Wilcox's Alabama brigade, Lang's Florida brigade, and Wright's Georgia brigade strike toward Cemetery Ridge. Several Union artillery batteries attempt to stall the Confederates. Wilcox's brigade is struck by the 1st Minnesota, and part of the 19th Maine. The 19th also hits Lang's brigade. With the help of Union infantry from Brewster's and Carr's infantry, and Lieutenant Evan Thomas' battery, Lang's brigade retreats.

Meanwhile, to Lang's left, Brigadier General Ambrose R. Wright's Georgia brigade, 1,413 men, advanced just south of the Copse of Trees. Union Lieutenant Alonzo Cushing's and Captain William A. Arnold's batteries sent an enfilading fire down Wright's left flank. Yet, due to the smoke, visibility became poor, and Brigadier General John Gibbon ordered the guns to cease firing.

With Lang's Florida brigade withdrawn, Colonel William R. Brewster's and Brigadier General Joseph Carr's Union troops then sent a volley down Wright's right flank. To make matters worse, the 13th Vermont charged into their right flank. Near the Copse of Trees, Wright's left flank was hit as well. The 69th Pennsylvania fired into the Georgia brigade's left. Union Brigadier General Alexander S. Webb then ordered his remaining regiments forward (see map 2). With great determination, the Union regiments pushed the Confederates back past the Emmitsburg Road, and recaptured several cannon. The fighting in the center of the Union line had ended. (Some Georgia infantrymen argued they advanced farther than Pickett's Virginians. It is, however, difficult to measure courage by feet.)

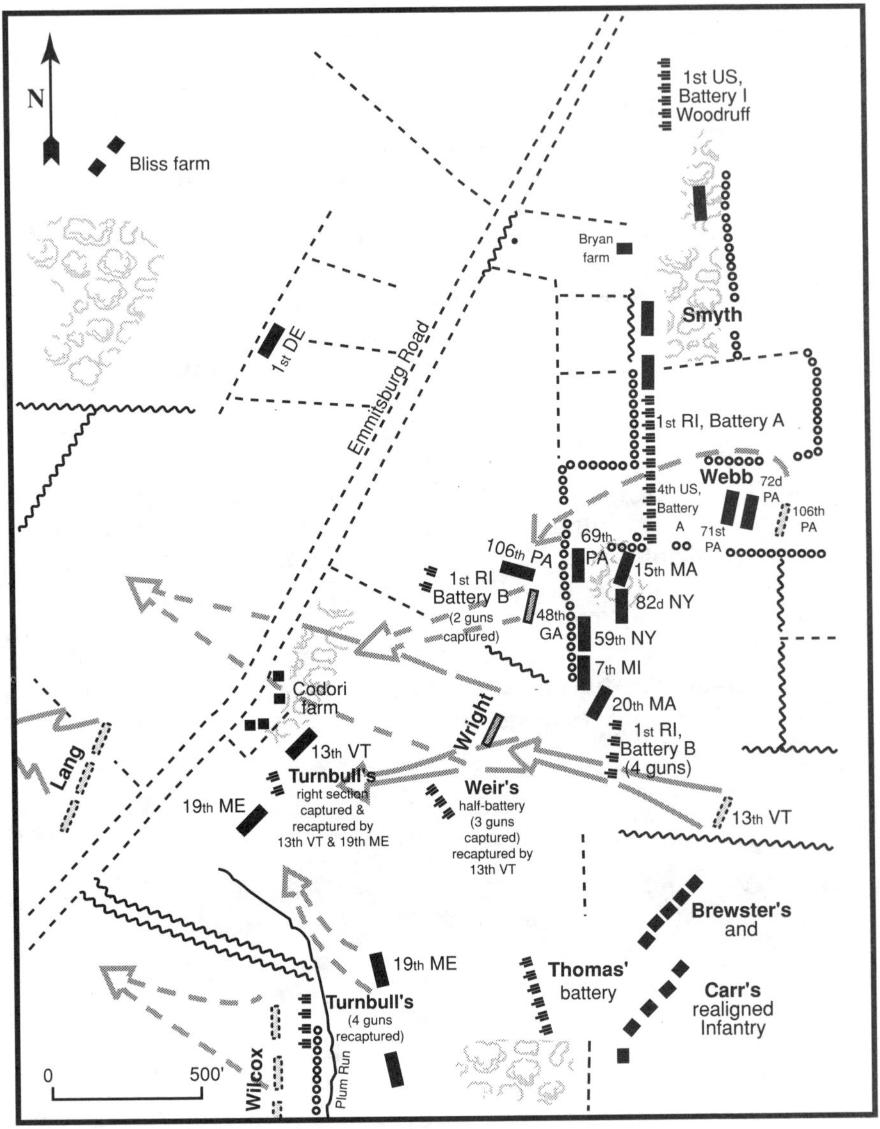

MAP 2

Stop 1: Intersection of Pleasonton and Hancock Avenues

Although Lang's and Wilcox's brigades retreat, Wright's continues and captures several Union artillery pieces. Brewster's and Carr's infantrymen fire into Wright's right flank; the 13th Vermont then charges. Near the Copse of Trees the 48th Georgia is hit by the 106th Pennsylvania. Taking fire on both flanks and the front, Wright's brigade withdraws back to Seminary Ridge. The Union infantry reclaim the captured cannon. Fighting ended around 7:30 p.m.

Summary of July 2

Union Major General George Meade directed a defensive position along Cemetery Ridge, Cemetery Hill, and Culp's Hill. General Lee planned to hit the Union line simultaneously on both flanks and in the center. After a hard day's fighting, the Confederates occupied the Peach Orchard/Devil's Den area, but failed to take Little Round Top, Culp's Hill, or East Cemetery Hill, essentially the high ground commanding the area.

A low estimate of casualties for the entire day (3:30 p.m.–12:00 a.m.) is 15,186 Americans either killed or wounded in nine-and-a-half hours (7,877 Union and 7,309 Confederates).

The Final Assault

"...if **Lee** ***attacked him tomorrow, he*** **(Lee)** ***would try the centre."***

–Major General George Gordon Meade

Friday, July 3

The Army of Northern Virginia:

Lee's initial strategy for July 3 was fairly simple. At dawn his troops on Culp's Hill would resume their attack. Simultaneously, three divisions under the command of Major General Isaac Trimble, Brigadier General J.J. Pettigrew and Major General George Pickett, 12,500 infantrymen, would strike Cemetery Hill and Cemetery Ridge—near the Copse of Trees. Meanwhile, Major General Jeb Stuart's cavalry, having arrived late at Gettysburg Thursday afternoon, would ride around the Union Army and strike at its rear (see map 3).

The Army of the Potomac:

Meade met with his subordinate generals Thursday night and decided to maintain the defensive position and await a Confederate assault. After the meeting Meade expressed his opinion to Brigadier General John Gibbon, his division deployed on Cemetery Ridge, that "...if *Lee* attacked him tomorrow, he (*Lee*) would try the centre."[2] The Union line was now shaped like a fishhook. Culp's Hill was the barb, Cemetery Hill the hook, and Cemetery Ridge the shank. Little Round Top/Big Round Top were an extension of the shank. During the morning of July 3, Meade and Hancock, in charge of the Union line on Cemetery Ridge, discussed the probability of an attack on the Union center.[3]

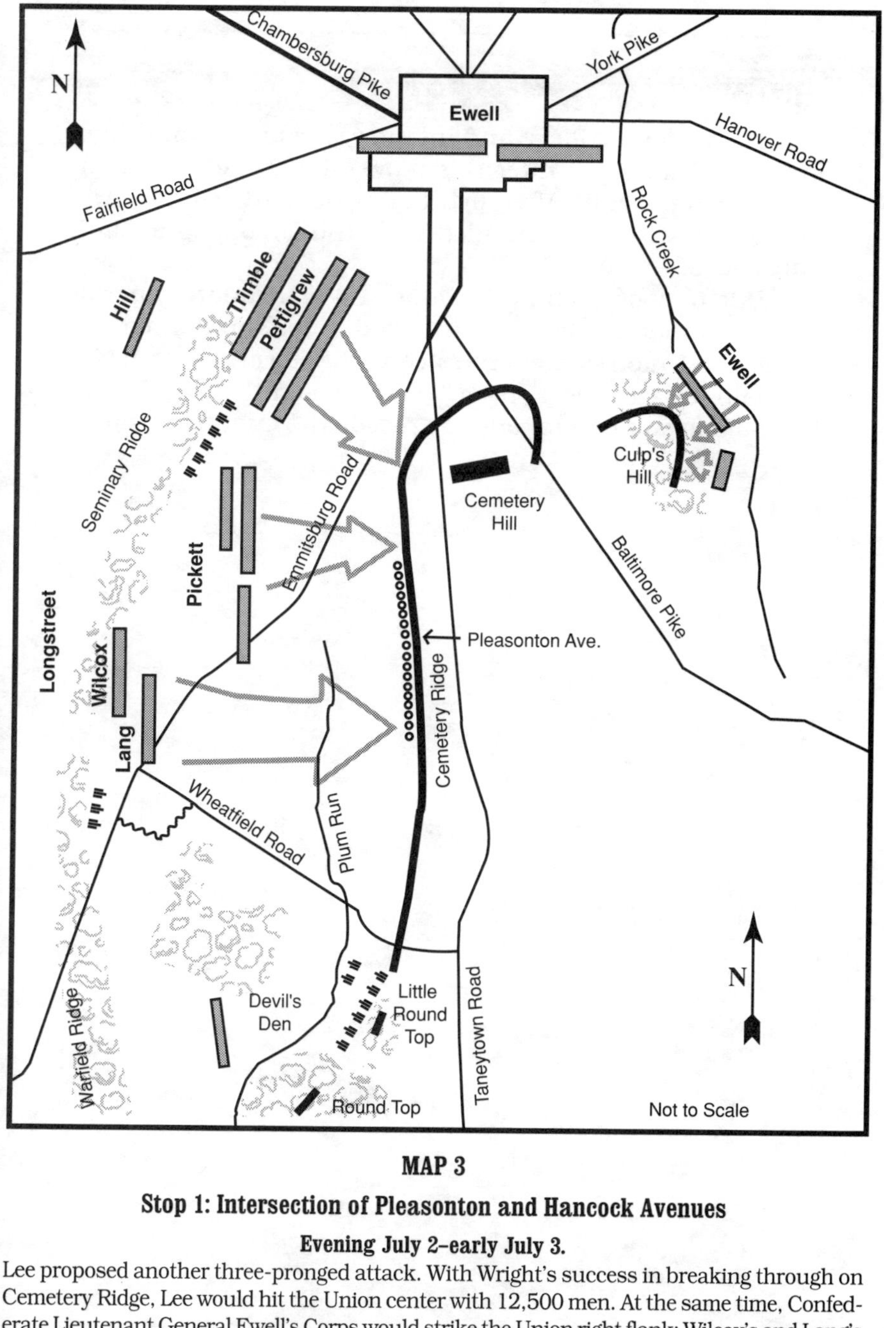

MAP 3

Stop 1: Intersection of Pleasonton and Hancock Avenues

Evening July 2–early July 3.

Lee proposed another three-pronged attack. With Wright's success in breaking through on Cemetery Ridge, Lee would hit the Union center with 12,500 men. At the same time, Confederate Lieutenant General Ewell's Corps would strike the Union right flank; Wilcox's and Lang's brigades would attack the Union left flank.

The Battle Resumes, Friday Morning

The Union artillery and infantry preempted an attack on Culp's Hill. To counter this move, the Confederates assaulted Culp's Hill. After five hours of hard fighting, the struggle for Culp's Hill ended with the Union right flank still secure.

Due to poor communications and inadequate generalship, the other Confederate troops did not simultaneously attack the Union center. Yet, Lee was determined to make his main assault there. In order to weaken the line, he ordered a massive cannonade to precede the infantry assault.

(Stay at the intersection.)

The Artillery Duel

July 3, 1:00–3:00 p.m.

"...frightened out of our wits..."

–Captain John Dooley

CONFEDERATE ARTILLERY COMMANDER:

Colonel E.P. Alexander, age 28
West Point graduate 1857, 3/38. At West Point he specialized in engineering. In 1862 he was given command of an artillery battalion. At Gettysburg, Longstreet put him in charge of the I Corps artillery.

USAMHI

UNION ARTILLERY COMMANDER:

Brigadier General Henry Hunt, age 44
Graduated from West Point 1839, 19/31. Wounded twice in the Mexican War. Forerunner in field artillery tactics, he became chief of artillery for the Army of the Potomac in '62. He was brevetted for his actions at Gettysburg.

USAMHI

Around 1:00 p.m., 142 cannon opened fire on the Union troops. In the northern section of the Confederate line 10 cannon concentrated their fire on the 29 cannon deployed on Cemetery Hill. In the center, 103 cannon opposed 31 Union guns. Near the Peach Orchard 28 cannon dueled with 43 Union cannon which were stationed from Little Round Top to the intersection of what is now the Pleasonton and

Hancock Avenues. The Union artillery reserve was positioned near Taneytown Road and was ready to replace damaged cannon along the line (see map 4).[4]

Lee hoped to demoralize the infantry on Cemetery Ridge and destroy the cannon. After disrupting the Union line, the Confederates planned for their infantry to break through the Union center, followed closely by reinforcements to smash the entire line.

The Union commanders attempted to destroy the Confederate guns, create havoc, and repulse the infantry assault.

Nearly 5,000 Union troops crowded in this area. They were hot in their wool uniforms and had little water or food. After the cannonade began, the entire valley filled with smoke, making visibility poor. Consequently, both artillery commands overshot their targets. One Union officer speculated that nine-tenths of the Confederate shells fell behind the infantry lines on Cemetery Ridge.[5] The men deployed on Cemetery Ridge, behind the stone wall, were actually safer than the men behind the ridge near Taneytown Road. Even so, the infantrymen lay close to the ground behind the stone wall and watched the projectiles pass overhead. The historian of the 19th Massachusetts wrote the following account:

> *...The rain of shot and shell was continous* [*sic*]. *Fragments of bursting shell were flying everywhere. There seemed to be no place where they did not strike and no spot from whence they did not come. Officers and men alike, keeping their alignment, crawled to places of apparent cover.*
>
> *...Men, lying flat behind large boulders, were struck. A shot would come over and strike a man in the back. Men were constantly seen hobbling off, with blood streaming from their wounds...*[6]

Near the Bryan farm, the 111th New York deployed and received an incoming shell which exploded in their midst killing seven.[7] The Union artillery returned fire. Caissons blew up; guns and their artillerymen were struck. Lieutenant Frank Haskell, of Gibbon's staff, wrote:

> *...a shell exploded over an open limber box in Cushing's Battery; and almost at the same instant,*

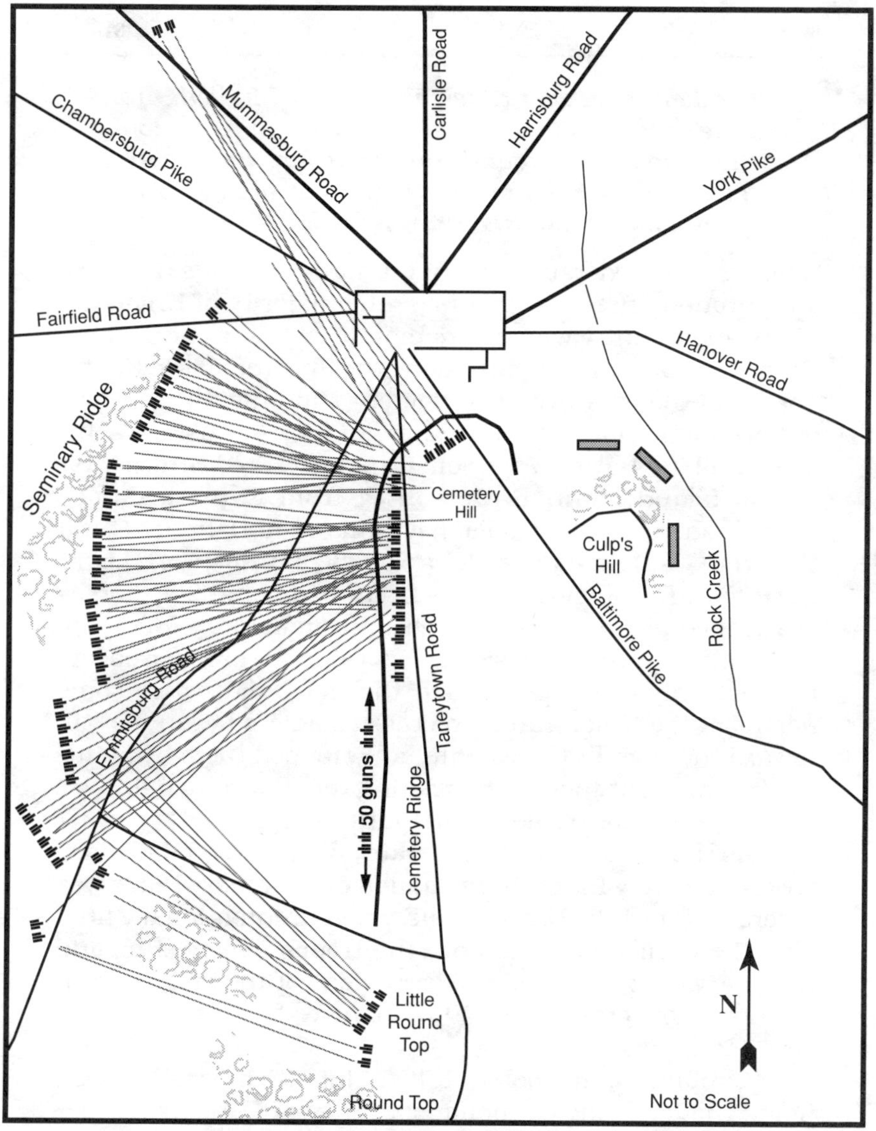

MAP 4

Stop 1: Intersection of Pleasonton and Hancock Avenues

The Artillery Duel, July 3, 1:00–3:00 p.m.

In order to demoralize the Union infantry, Lee ordered a huge cannonade to proceed the final assault. Approximately 261 guns participated in the two-hour duel. The entire area was soon engulfed in smoke. Confederate artillerymen concentrated mostly on Cemetery Ridge and Hill. The Union cannon deployed on the southern edge of Cemetery Ridge are ordered not to fire so that they do not expose their positions. Artillerymen on both sides overshoot their targets.

> *another shell, over a neighboring box. In both the boxes the ammunition blew up with an explosion that shook the ground, throwing fire, and splinters, and shells far into the air and all around, and destroying several men.*[8]

While the Confederate artillery hit many caissons, limbers, ammunition chests, and horses, the majority of Union artillery and infantry were not demoralized in the cannonade. Of the approximate 87 guns along the line from Little Round Top to Ziegler's Grove on Cemetery Hill only 14 were put out of commission: 4 from Lieutenant Alonzo Cushing's 4th U.S. Artillery, Battery A; 3 from Captain T. Fred Brown's 1st Rhode Island Light, Battery B; 4 from Captain James Thompson's consolidated Pennsylvania Light Batteries C and F; 3 from Captain James McKay Rorty, 1st New York Light, Battery B. One regimental historian estimated 250 horses were killed or wounded during the cannonade.[9]

Although the explosion of caissons and limber chests harmed only a few personnel, the noise did cause some nerves in the Union ranks to crack. Soldiers began to walk toward the rear, but one lieutenant stopped them by pointing his sword at them and ordering them to return to their posts.[10] The infantrymen reluctantly complied.

As the majority of Confederate shells missed the infantry on Cemetery Ridge, the situation on Seminary Ridge was reversed. Since the Union artillerymen unintentionally fired over the Confederate cannon, the troops deployed behind Seminary Ridge, in the woods in front of the ridge and in the open, low ground near the Spangler farm, suffered severe casualties.

Captain John Dooley, 1st Virginia (Kemper's brigade) noted the terrifying cannonade:

> *...the air is shaking from earth to sky with every missile of death fired from the cannon's mouth. Around, above, beneath, and on all sides they schreech [sic], sing, scream, whistle, roar, whirr, buzz, bang and whizz, and we are obliged to lie quietly tho' frightened out of our wits and unable to do any thing in our defence or any injury to our enemies.*[11]

To the 1st Virginia's left the 7th Virginia hugged the earth. Sergeant Major David E. Johnston, 7th Virginia (Kemper's brigade), recalled the scene:

> *The sun, but a moment before so brilliant, was now almost darkened by smoke and mist enveloping and shadowing the earth, and through which came hissing and shrieking, fiery fuses and messengers of death, sweeping, plunging, cutting, ploughing through our ranks, carrying mutilation, destruction, pain, suffering and death in every direction. Turn your eyes whithersoever you would, and there was to be seen at almost every moment of time, guns, swords, haversacks, human flesh and bones, flying and dangling in the air, or bouncing above the earth...Over us, in front of us, behind us, and in our midst, and through our ranks, poured death on every hand...*[12]

Johnston found himself near an apple tree. Colonel Walter Tazewell Patton, 7th Virginia, Colonel Joseph Mayo, 3d Virginia, and Lieutenant James Brown, 7th Virginia, also lay nearby. (Colonel Patton was an ancestor of the World War II General George Patton. During the assault Colonel W.T. Patton was shot through the mouth and mortally wounded.) As the Union shelling slackened, Johnston raised his head a little in order to take a breath of fresh air. Brown then stated to him, "you had better put your head down or you may get it knocked off."

Johnston replied, "well, Lieut., a man had as about as well die that way as to suffocate for want of air." Just about that moment an explosion occurred right over their heads. Johnston described the gruesome site. "...Around me were brains, blood and skull bones; my first thought was that my Colonel's head had been blown off." His colonel, however, had survived the blast, but the two soldiers to Johnston's left had their heads blown away just over the ears. Lieutenant Brown was also severely wounded. The explosion broke several of Johnston's ribs and bruised his left lung; he lay out of action.[13]

Lieutenant John Lewis, 9th Virginia (Armistead's brigade), remembered the terrifying cannonade:

> *....Man seldom ever sees or hears the like of this but once in a lifetime; and those that saw and heard this infernal crash and witnessed the havoc made by the shrieking, howling missiles of death as they plowed the earth and tore the trees will never forget it. It seemed that death was in every foot of space, and safety was only in flight; but none of the men did that. To know the tension of mind under a fire like that, it must be experienced; it can not be told in words. There is nothing to which I could compare it so as it would be made plain to one who had never been there.*[14]

Over in Pettigrew and Trimble's divisions the scene took on the same horror. A cannon shot struck Jeremiah S. Gage of Company A, 11th Mississippi. It nearly tore off his left arm between the elbow and shoulder and cut through his lower abdomen, carrying away his bladder, much of his intestine, and a third of the right half of his pelvis. As he lay dying the boy penned one last letter to his mother:

> *This is the last you may ever hear from me. I have time to tell you that I died like a man. Bear my loss best you can. Remember that I am true to my country and my greatest regret at dying is that she is not free and that you and my sisters are robbed of my worth whatever that may be. I hope this will reach you and you must not regret that my body can not be obtained. It is a mere matter of form anyhow. This is for my sisters too as I can not write more. Send my dying release to Miss Mary...you know who.*
>
> *J.S. Gage*
> *Mrs. P.W. Gage* *Co. A, 11th Miss.*
> *Richland,*
> *Holmes County*
> *Miss.*
>
> *This letter is stained with my blood.*[15]

Around 1:25 p.m., fearing they might run out of ammunition, Colonel Edward P. Alexander, chief of artillery for the Confederate First Corps, penned a note to Major General Pickett, "If you are coming at all you must come at once, or I cannot give you proper support, but the enemy's fire has not slackened at all. At least 18 guns are still firing from the cemetery itself."[16] (Alexander's watch may have been off by an hour-and-a-half for the cannonade lasted until around 3:00 p.m.) About ten minutes later he sent another message, "For God's sake come quick. The 18 guns are gone. Come quick or I can't support you."[17]

What 18 guns Alexander mentioned in his message is a mystery to historians.[18] No 18 guns ever left the Union line at one time or even piecemeally. The cannon, however, on Cemetery Ridge did slacken and cease fire after two hours on Meade's orders. He believed the cannon were doing little harm to the Confederate guns and were simply creating more smoke in the valley.[19] Also, Brigadier General Henry J. Hunt, chief of artillery, wanted to conserve ammunition for the impending charge. In addition, Meade, Hunt, Major Thomas W. Osborn, chief of artillery for the XI Corps and the XI Corps commander, Major General Oliver O. Howard, hoped to lure the Confederate infantry to attack.[20] In order to prepare for the infantry assault new guns replaced the badly damaged cannon. As the battered batteries retired, the Confederates saw the guns being removed but were unaware of their replacements. (Alexander may have noted damaged Union artillery limbering up and falling back. Yet, he did not seem to see the replacements deploying.)

Go to Stop 2: Vermont Monuments (see map 5)

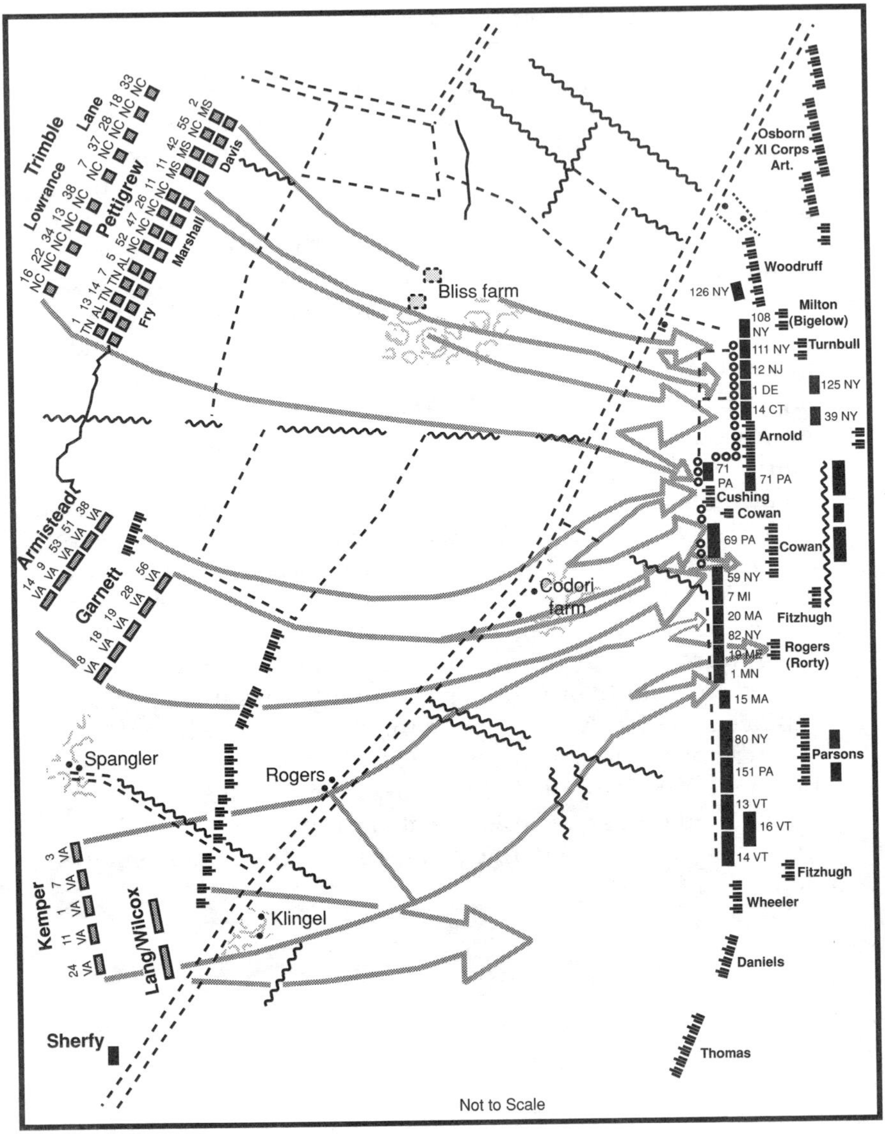

MAP 5

Stop 2: Vermont Monuments

The Advance, 3:00–3:30 p.m.

In order to avoid colliding with Garnett's brigade, Kemper's started marching south-east toward Little Round Top. At the Emmitsburg Road, Kemper's brigade made a complicated oblique left and advanced toward the Copse of Trees. Over on the Confederate left, Pettigrew's brigades, which had suffered heavy losses on the first day, deployed their regiments into two

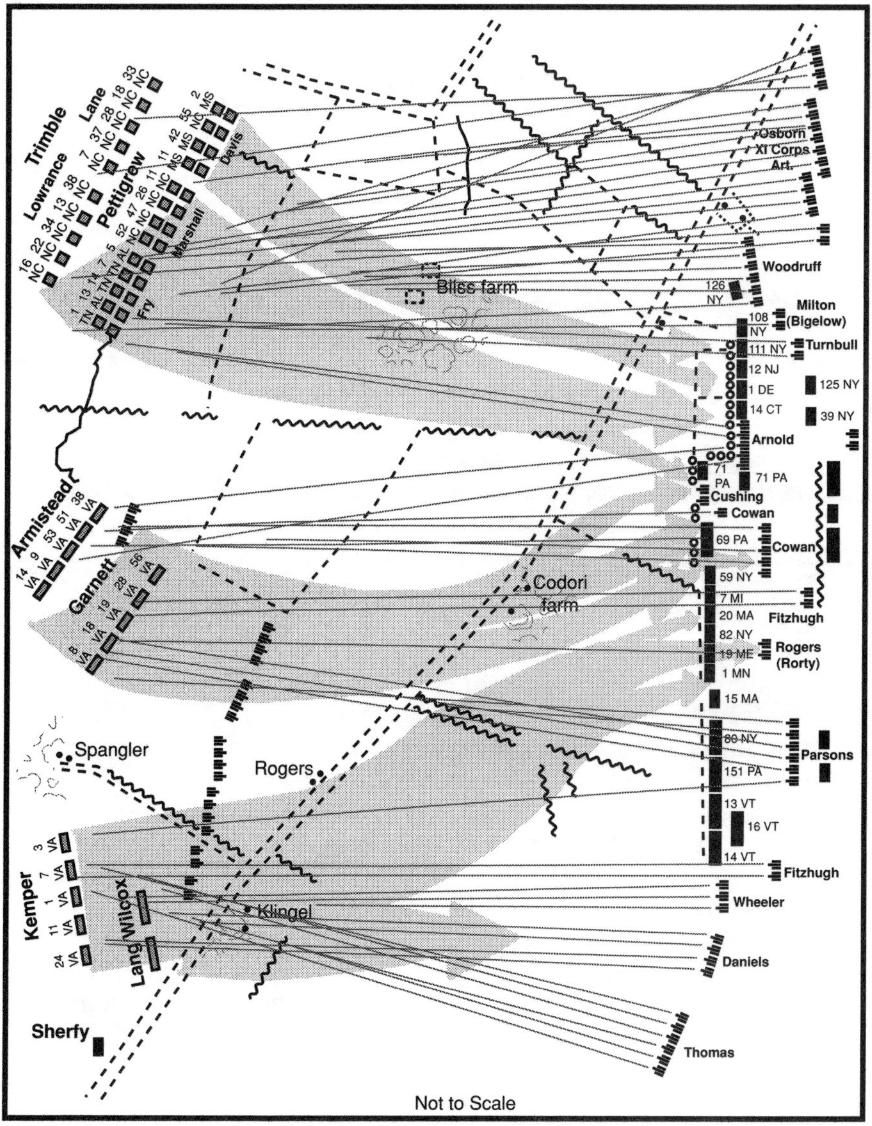

lines. Trimble's regiments stationed themselves behind Pettigrew and in one line. While advancing across the mile-wide, open field, over 100 Union cannon stationed from Little Round Top to Cemetery Hill catch the Confederate infantry in a terrible crossfire.

Vermont Monuments

The Advance

"I shall lead my division forward."

—Major General George Pickett

3:00–3:30 p.m.

Upon receiving the message from Alexander, Pickett moved quickly to find his corps commander, Lieutenant General Longstreet, to ask his approval to move out. Feeling that the attack was ill advised, Longstreet merely bowed his head. Pickett then saluted and said, "I shall lead my division forward, sir."[1]

Three Confederate division commanders participated in the final assault: Major General George Pickett, Brigadier General James J. Pettigrew, and Major General Isaac Trimble—18 Virginia regiments, 15 North Carolina regiments, 3 Mississippi regiments, 2 Alabama regiments, and 2 Tennessee regiments, a total of 12,500 infantrymen (see map 5).[2]

Pickett's division had not been involved in a major engagement since the spring of 1862. His men, therefore, were eager to share in the glory which other units had earned. Pickett was also anxious to command his grand division in this attack; however, he had never before commanded a division in combat. His division attacked the southern end of Cemetery Ridge to the stone wall where it makes a 90º angle. On the other side of the angle, near Bryan's farm and Cemetery Hill, Pettigrew and Trimble's men struck.

The Union infantry in this area numbered around 5,750.[3]

Opposing Commanders:

CONFEDERATE:

First Corps
Lieutenant General
James Longstreet

Division Commander
Pickett's division, First Corps
Major General George Pickett

(4,800)*

Brigade Commander
Kemper's brigade, Pickett's division, First Corps
Brigadier General
James Kemper

1st Va., 3d Va., 7th Va.,
11th Va., 24th Va.
(1,325)

UNION:

I Corps
Major General
Abner Doubleday

and

II Corps
Major General Winfield Hancock

Division Commander
Third Division, I Corps
Brigadier General
Thomas Rowley
(1,400)

Brigade Commander
3d Brigade, Third Division, I Corps
Brigadier General
George Stannard

13th Vt., 14th Vt.,
16th Vt.
(1,400)

Division Commander
Second Division, II Corps
Brigadier General John Gibbon
(3,785)†

Brigade Commanders
1st Brigade, Second Division, II Corps
Brigadier General
William Harrow
19th Maine, 15th Mass.,
1st Minn., 82d N.Y.
(700)

3d Brigade, Second Division, II Corps
Colonel Norman J. Hall
19th Mass., 20th Mass.,
7th Mich., 42d and 59th N.Y.
(570)

* Pickett's division had suffered heavy casualties during the cannonade.

† This number includes three Vermont regiments and two other Union regiments which were not in Gibbon's division but were stationed on Cemetery Ridge. In this area up to the Copse of Trees approximately 1,325 Confederates fought against 3,215 Union infantrymen.

Once Pickett obtained permission to begin the attack he rode down his division shouting, "...up men, and to your posts! Don't forget today you are from old Virginia."[4] The soldiers unharmed in the cannonade jumped up and fell in. Many Confederates waved to their comrades who had been wounded during the shelling and shouted, "Goodbye, boys! Goodbye!"[5]

To the Union soldiers the huge mass of infantrymen resembled a gray ocean tide.[6] When they moved into the open field, approximately 103 Union cannon on Cemetery Hill, Ridge and Little Round Top fired into the infantrymen. Shot, shell, spherical case, shrapnel and canister, thousands of deadly missiles raced through the air to thin the Confederate ranks. A projectile exploded in front of a regiment killing three men and wounding five others. "Close up, men!" someone shouted, and the gap disappeared as soldiers took the place of the dead and wounded. An officer's head was shattered by a round shot, but his men simply stepped over the body. Again an officer shouted, "Close up!"—"Not too fast on the left"—"Major, take command, the Colonel is down," as they continued through the brutal storm of shot and shell.[7] One soldier dropped, announcing he was wounded. When his sergeant demanded to see the wound, the young man ran away. The sergeant followed but lost him in the crowd.[8] Captain John Dooley, 1st Virginia, vividly described the trying time:

> *...the bravest of the brave are sinking to rise no more! Still onward! Capt. Hallinan has fallen and I take his place. So many men have fallen now that I find myself within a few feet of my old Captain (Norton)...Still we press on—oh, how long it seems before we reach those blazing guns. Our men falling faster now, for the deadly musket is at work. Volley after volley of crashing musket balls sweeps through the line and mow us down like wheat before the scythe.*[9]

All along the lines Confederates suffered heavy casualties as they continued their relentless advance across that fateful mile.

Collision

"...determined to slay the very last man..."

–Private Ralph O. Sturtevant

After crossing the Emmitsburg Road, Brigadier General James Kemper's brigade drifted to the left concentrating on the Copse of Trees. Captain Dooley fell about thirty yards from the Union line, shot through both thighs. (Dooley was later captured; he survived his wounds.)

By moving to the left Kemper's right flank was exposed. Brigadier General George Stannard seized this opportunity and sent two Vermont regiments, the 13th and the 16th, into his flank. The deadly cross fire hit the Confederates, and then the Vermonters rushed them with bayonets. Private Ralph O. Sturtevant, 13th Vermont, recalled the battle:

> *As the 13th charged forward from its last position where it had been pouring in volley after volley at short range from musket and pistol...realizing...that some of the more revengeful and desperate continued to fire in our faces as we advanced. We opened fire again and then rushed up against them with bayonets pushed forward revengefully determined to slay the very last man unless they would heed their proffered offer of surrender. Bayonets crossed and the desperate thrusts exchanged, and the hand to hand struggle followed. Many fell wounded and bleeding pierced with bayonet, sword, and pistol musket balls...*[10]

Kemper fell from his horse, shot through the body, the bullet exiting near his groin. The Vermonters captured him, but he was quickly retaken by his own men.[11] Once the Confederates began surrendering, Colonel Francis Voltaire Randall, commander of the 13th Vermont, at his own risk, passed rapidly down the front of his regiment shouting, "Stop firing!"[12]

Hancock was with Stannard when the Vermonters struck the enemy column. Hancock fell from his horse; a bullet had pierced the pummel of his saddle and entered his groin. The minié ball also drove a nail from his saddle into his groin. He was carried to a field hospital; remarkably, he survived his wound.[13]

After striking Kemper's right flank, the 16th Vermont faced about and charged into the Confederate reinforcements (Wilcox's and Lang's brigades). With the help of the 14th Vermont and Union artillery (59 guns) on the southern end of Cemetery Ridge and Little Round Top the two brigades turned back (see map 6).[14]

Captain John Dooley, age 21
Company C, 1st Virginia. Shot through both thighs; survived his wounds.
John Dooley: Confederate Soldier His War Journal

Private Ralph Orson Sturtevant, age 25
Company K, 13th Vermont.
Pictorial History of the Thirteenth Regiment Vermont Volunteers, War of 1861–1865

Go to Stop 3: Cemetery Ridge, Monument of 1st Independent New York Light Artillery Battery, Cowan's battery

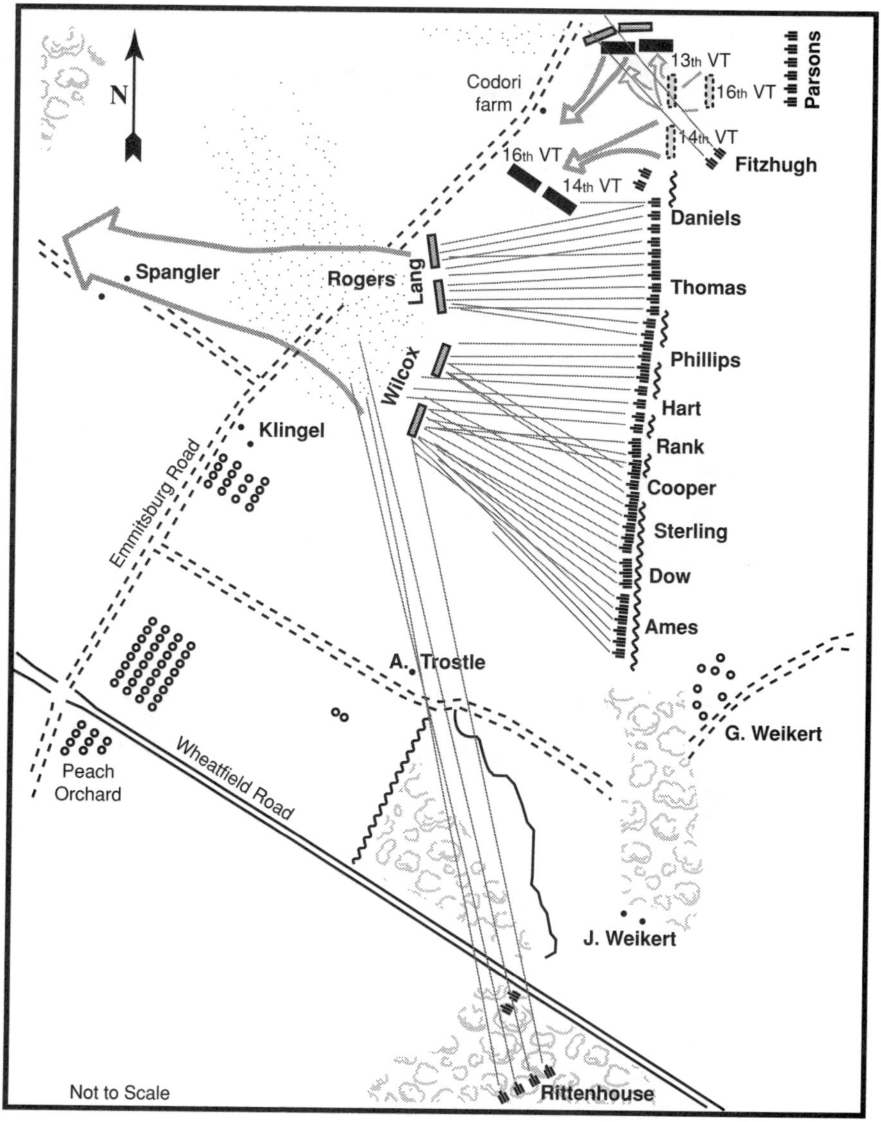

MAP 6

Stop 2: Vermont Monuments

Collision

As Kemper's brigade concentrates on the Copse of Trees, his right flank is exposed. The 13th Vermont and 16th Vermont make a right face and fire into this flank. About twenty minutes after the main assault began, Lang's and Wilcox's brigades attack the Union right flank. They are summarily stopped by 59 Union guns stationed on the southern end of Cemetery Ridge and Little Round Top. The 16th Vermont and 14th Vermont also charge into the two Confederate brigades. Some men in the 14th Vermont are hit by Union artillery fire.

Stop 3

Cemetery Ridge, near Monument of 1st Independent New York Light Artillery Battery, Cowan's Battery.

"...Perfectly redicklous [sic]..."

–Confederate captain 3d Virginia

The Virginians on Kemper's right flank attempted to ignore the Vermonters and concentrate on the Copse of Trees. Colonel Joseph J. Mayo, 3d Virginia, actually remembered some scenes which amused him:

> *...While clearing this obstruction* [the Codori farm], *and as we were getting into shape again, several things were impressed on my memory. First, the amusement it seemed to afford Orderly Waddy Forward, who might, if he pleased, have stayed behind with the horses, to see me duck my head as a ball whizzed in an ace of my nose; next, to see Captain Lewis, of Company C, looking as lazy and lackadaisical, and, if possible, more tired and bored than usual, carrying his sword point foremost over his shoulder, and addressing his company in that invariable plaintive tone, half command, half entreaty, "Don't crowd, boys; don't crowd."* [Colonel Mayo shouted] *"Pretty hot, Captain," "It's redicklous* [sic], *Colonel; perfectly redicklous* [sic]*..."*[1]

The impetuous will of Kemper's right flank breached the stone wall. Private Lucas L. Meredith, Company C, 3d Virginia carried the battle flag for his company. The Union regiments, weakened from the second day's fighting, broke.

Captain Andrew Cowan's New York battery (five guns) unlimbered behind the infantrymen. The artillerymen were disgusted and angered by the Union infantry's retreat. Cowan later wrote of the incident:

> *...General Hunt, who was in my battery after I opened with canister, was very fearful that my fire*

would damage our own men, but I was on foot and could see what we were doing better than the general mounted. He emptied his pistol at the enemy as I was loading for the third round. Just then the (Union) infantry in front of five of my guns wavered and was about to give way when General Webb rushed from the right and drew them off behind Cushing's guns. A great many men, however, ran back through my guns and I saw several officers running away. Corporal Plunkett struck one man over the head with a coffee pot and it went down over his face, the bottom giving way, and in that plight he ran off with it. Some of the rebels came on and crossed the wall (then almost demolished and nowhere over a foot high in my front). Then I fired my last canister. One rebel, a Major I thought, was killed by my fire within a few feet of the gun. [Cowan later buried the officer.][2]

Surging once again through this small crack, the Virginians met a thunderous roar from Cowan's five guns, which spewed double-shotted canister. The blast cut wagon-sized gaps in their line. When the smoke cleared, not one Confederate remained standing. In some places their mutilated bodies lay three deep (see map 7).[3]

Private Lucas L. Meredith
Company C, 3d Virginia. Carried the company battle flag. Survived the battle, died in 1927.
GNMP (Gettysburg National Military Park) (Postwar)

Captain Andrew Cowan, age 22
1st New York Light Independent Battery.
USAMHI

Go to Stop 4: "The Angle"

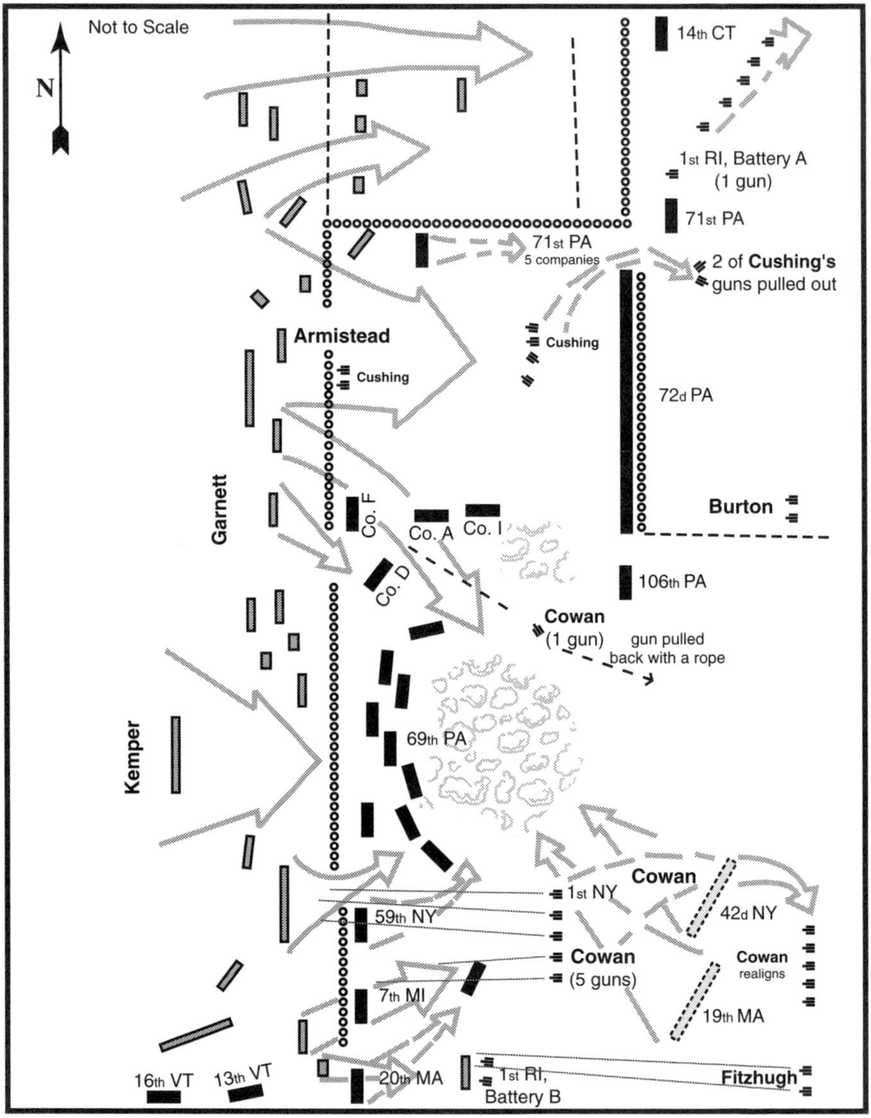

MAP 7

Stops 3 and 4: Cowan's battery and the "Angle"

(The Union and Confederate lines were not this well-defined; soldiers blindly fired at one another.) While the Vermont regiments hit Kemper's right, squads of Confederates break through the Union line on his left flank. Cowan's five guns spew double-canister. Some Union infantry are hit as well. Near the "Angle" Armistead, with about 200 men, smashes the Union line. The 69th Pennsylvania's right flank attempts to re-fuse their line. Armistead continues toward the abandoned cannon. He falls mortally wounded near one of the guns. About thirty Confederates lie near their general.

Stop 4

"The Angle"

"...give 'em the cold steel, boys."

–Brigadier General Lewis Armistead

Opposing Commanders:

CONFEDERATE:

Brigade Commanders
Garnett's brigade, Pickett's division, First Corps

Brigadier General
Richard B. Garnett
8th Va., 18th Va., 19th Va.,
28th Va., 56th Va.
(1,405)

Armistead's brigade,
Pickett's division, First Corps

Brigadier General Lewis Armistead
9th Va., 14th Va., 38th Va.,
53d Va., 57th Va.
(1,570)*

UNION:

Brigade Commander
2d Brigade, Second Division, II Corps

Brigadier General
Alexander Webb
69th Pa., 71st Pa., 72d Pa.,
106th Pa.
(880)

At the Angle, the 69th Pennsylvania and five companies from the 71st Pennsylvania were deployed. They became the focal point of Garnett's and Armistead's brigades. Garnett's Virginians hit the Pennsylvanians first. Major Charles Peyton, commander of the 19th Virginia, was the only regimental leader who was not killed or wounded.

> *Our line, much shattered, still kept up the advance until within about 20 paces of the wall, when, for a moment, it recoiled under the terrific fire that poured into our ranks both from the batteries and from their sheltered infantry. At this moment, General*

---

* Initially 2,895 Confederates confronted 880 Union soldiers in this area, but the two Confederate brigades suffered heavy casualties while advancing across the open field.

Kemper came up on the right and General Armistead in rear, when the three lines, joining in concert, rushed forward with unyielding determination and an apparent spirit laudable rivalry to plant the Southern banner on the walls of the enemy. His strongest and last line was instantly gained.[1]

The Angle: Looking toward Seminary Ridge.
This is where Armistead and about two hundred Confederates broke through.

With the entire area engulfed in smoke and deafening noise, men from the 69th and 71st Pennsylvania soon found rifles against their chests; flames from the gun powder discharge burned the men's clothes. The Confederate musket fire was frightfully effective. Colonel Dennis O'Kane, commander of the 69th Pennsylvania, was shot through the chest; he died July 5. A minié ball struck Lieutenant Colonel Martin Tschudy in the bladder, and he fell dead; a bullet struck Private William Hayes in the head, and he toppled.[2] Under the weight of the attack the 69th's right flank refused their line. Company D held the enemy at bay with clubbed muskets. The 69th's historian later recounted the melée:

> *...Corporal* [Hugh] *Bradley, of this company* [D], *a powerful man, was using his piece as a club very effectively, but was overpowered by numbers and had his skull crushed by a blow from a musket in the hands of a rebel.*[3]

Another Confederate from the 28th Virginia "dispatched [a Union soldier] with his bayonet."[4]

On the left side of the Pennsylvania regiment two cannon had been placed at the wall. Lieutenant Alonzo Cushing commanded these guns, and the other four behind him. Already wounded in the shoulder and groin, he was shot through the mouth and killed and lay dead next to one of his guns.[5] With no infantry support, the artillerymen abandoned the two guns near the wall. Virginians from Garnett's and Armistead's brigades surged through the breach. Garnett had been killed, but Armistead led approximately two hundred Confederates over the wall. Adjutant James Crocker, 9th Virginia, Armistead's brigade, described the desperate assault:

> *...Our flag is planted on the defenses. Victory seems within grasp, but more is to be done. Brave Armistead, coming up, overleaps the wall and calls on all to follow. Brave men follow his lead. Armistead is now among the abandoned cannon, making ready to turn them against their former friends. Our men are widening the breach of the penetrated and broken lines of the Federals. But, now the enemy has made a stand, and are rallying. It is a critical moment...Armistead is shot down with mortal wounds and heavy slaughter is made of those around him. The final moment has come when there must be instant flight, instant surrender, or instant death.*[6]

Lieutenant J. Irving Sale, of the 53d Virginia, Armistead's brigade, also remembered those grave moments:

> *It was awful the way the men dropped. When we got right up here a few feet from the stone wall you fellows were behind, we all lay down and blazed away at the top of the wall wherever we could see a head. You blazed back so hard that in about a*

minute we gave that up and rushed over the wall. General Armistead was right ahead of me...When we poured over the wall, he waved his hat and sword and yelled: 'Now give 'em the cold steel, boys.' Yes, I was only a few feet behind him when he fell...I never saw so many dead men in my life as there were here. The blue coats were lying all over so thick that you could scarcely help stepping on them.[7]

Armistead continued toward the Union line; near Cushing's other four cannon he fell, shot in the leg and arm (see map 7). (In a space of not more than seven feet a war correspondent counted seven dead. Three were piled on top of one another. Nearby, in a space of approximately fifteen square feet, lay fifteen bodies. The Union soldiers counted approximately forty-two dead Confederates in the Angle.)[8]

Brigadier General Richard B. Garnett, age 46
West Point graduate 1841, 29/52. Shot and killed instantly.
USAMHI

Brigadier General Lewis Armistead, age 46
Expelled from West Point for breaking a plate over Jubal Early's head. Hit in the leg and arm; died July 5. Before he died he spitefully said to the Union doctor, "Men who can subsist on raw corn, can never be whipped."[9]
USAMHI

Lieutenant Alonzo Cushing, age 22
West Point graduate 1861, 12/34. Hit in the shoulder, groin and then shot through the mouth.
USAMHI

Go to Stop 5: Copse of Trees

Stop 5

Copse of Trees

"...they blindly plied the work of slaughter..."

–19th Massachusetts' regimental historian

To counter this threat the Union troops, who had scattered at the wall, were re-formed. Officers in this area drew their swords and yelled, "halt," "face about," and, "fire." Those soldiers who did not quickly obey were slapped with the flat of the sabre. Assimilated into the second line, 12 Union regiments from Pennsylvania, Maine, Massachusetts, Michigan, Minnesota, and New York fired at the onrushing Virginians (see map 8).[1] The regimental historian of the 19th Massachusetts wrote the following chilling account as the two lines collided:

> *...Foot to foot, body to body and man to man they struggled, pushed, and strived and killed. Each had rather die than yield. The mass of wounded and heaps of dead entangled the feet of the contestants, and, underneath the trampling mass, wounded men who could no longer stand, struggled, fought shouted and killed—hatless, coatless, drowned in sweat, black with powder, and blind with dust, with fiendish yells and strange oaths they blindly plied the work of slaughter.*[2]

Soldiers from the 19th Maine also pushed their way into the second Union line.

> *...Then such a scene as followed. We were all loading and firing and yelling and pushing towards the gap now filled with the exultant rebels. Company, regimental and brigade organizations were lost, and we were a great crowd. We would load, run to the front and fire, then others would jump in front of us and fire, and the color bearers, always at the front, would toss their colors up and down to show the enemy that we were not going to give*

> *it up, and to encourage us on. I got a cartridge in wrong end first, and the only man of my regiment I could see fired off his rammer. He and I kept together. The ground was covered with arms of every description, and we had no difficulty in supplying ourselves. And so we kept on and on—then suddenly I found myself rushing with all our crowd upon the enemy with an impetuosity that was irresistible, and the day was ours. Many of the rebels fled; but thousands...were captured.*[3]

The sorely outnumbered Confederates either retreated or surrendered.

Go to Stop 6: Cannon of 1st Rhode Island Light Artillery, Battery A

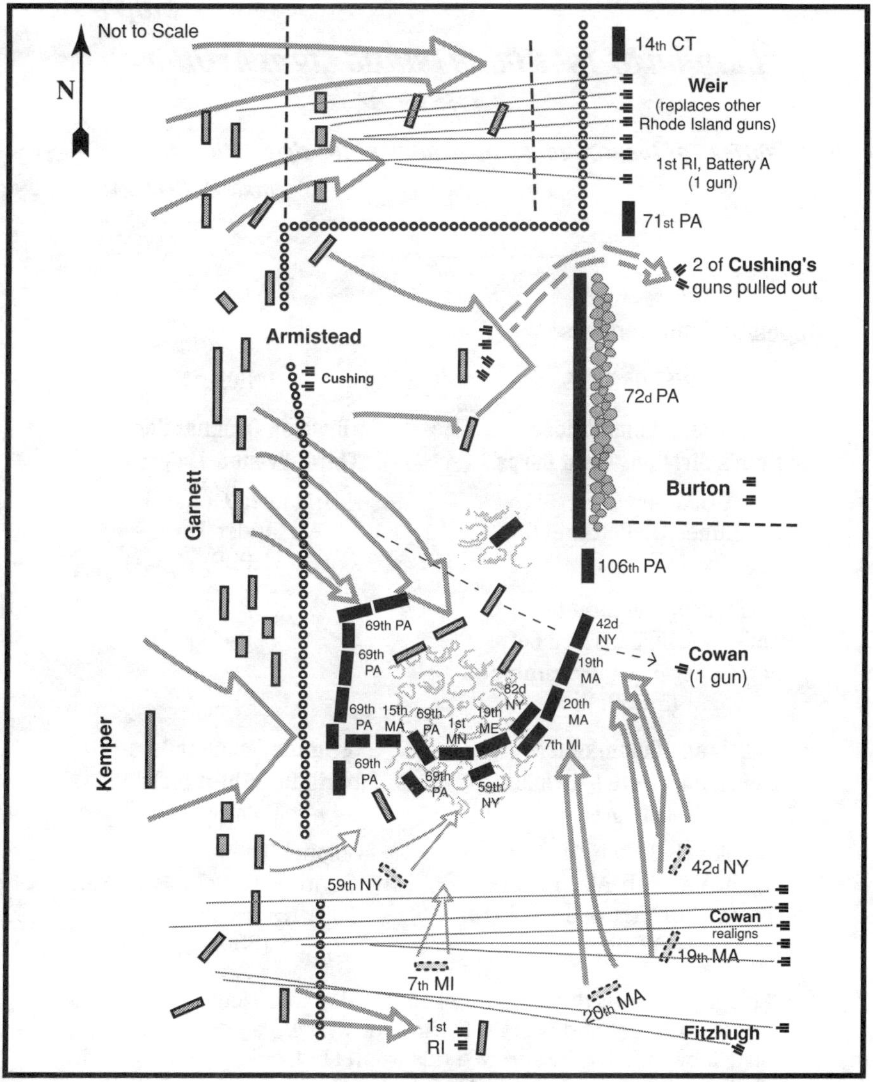

MAP 8

Stop 5: Copse of Trees

(The Union and Confederate lines were not this well-defined; soldiers blindly fired at one another.)
Some Confederates overrun two cannon from 1st Rhode Island, Battery B. Cowan's five guns withdraw and realign at the crest of Cemetery Ridge. With the help of two guns from Captain Robert Fitzhugh's battery, Cowan fires into Kemper's right flank again. The Union regiments, through which Kemper's brigade had broken, realign near the Copse of Trees. Other regiments are rushed in as reinforcements. A few Confederates enter the Copse of Trees.

Stop 6

Cannon of 1st Rhode Island Light Artillery, Battery A

"...shrieks of the wounded and groans of the dying filled the air..."

–Private Charles D. Page

Opposing Commanders:

CONFEDERATE

Division Commander
Heth's division, Third Corps

*Brigadier General
James J. Pettigrew

Division Commander
Pender's division, Third Corps

†Major General Isaac Trimble
(5,600)

Brigade Commanders
3d Brigade, Heth's division, Third Corps

‡Colonel Birkett D. Fry
13th Ala., 5th Ala. Batt.,
1st Tenn., 7th Tenn., 14th Tenn.
(900)

UNION

Division Commander
Third Division, II Corps

Brigadier General
Alexander Hays
(1,920)

Brigade Commanders
2d Brigade, Third Division, II Corps

§Colonel Thomas Smyth
14th Conn., 1st Del., 12th N.J.,
10th N.Y., 108th N.Y.
(830)

* Pettigrew assumed command of Heth's division. Heth was wounded on the first day and was ill. During the attack Pettigrew's hand was struck by canister; he survived this wound but was mortally wounded during a rear-guard skirmish, July 14. He died July 17.

† Near Emmitsburg Road Major General Trimble was wounded in the left leg by a bullet. He survived his injury but was later captured.

‡ During the cannonade, Colonel Fry was hit in the shoulder from a shell fragment. He stayed with his command.

§ Smyth was wounded in the face; however, he remained with his command.

1st Brigade, Heth's division, Third Corps

*Colonel J.K. Marshall
11th N.C., 26th N.C., 47th N.C., 52d N.C.
(1,500)

4th Brigade, Heth's division, Third Corps

Brigadier General Joseph Davis
2d Miss., 11th Miss., 42d Miss., 55th N.C.

2d Brigade, Heth's division, Third Corps

Colonel J.M. Brockenbrough
40th Va., 47th Va., 55th Va., 22d Va. Batt.

2d Brigade, Pender's division, Third Corps

Brigadier General James Lane
7th N.C. 18th N.C., 28th N.C., 33d N.C., 37th N.C.
(1,200)

4th Brigade, Pender's division, Third Corps

Colonel W. Lee J. Lowrance
13th N.C., 16th N.C., 22d N.C., 34th N.C., 38th N.C.
(500)

3d Brigade, Third Division, II Corps

†Colonel Eliakim Sherrill
39th N.Y., 111th N.Y., 125th N.Y., 126th N.Y.
(930)

* Col. James K. Marshall assumed command of Pettigrew's brigade when Pettigrew received a field promotion to Pender's division. Marshall, shot through the body, fell from his horse dead.

† Shot in the abdomen and killed during the attack on July 3.

Although the Confederates initially outnumbered the Union troops in this area, they suffered heavily during their advance.

To the right of the Angle, near the wall, the Confederates struggled to reach the crest. Captain William A. Arnold, 1st Rhode Island Light Artillery, Battery A was about to be overrun. Arnold quickly ordered his battery out by piece (meaning each gun and their artillerymen pulled back one by one. This tactic allowed covering fire for the retreating cannoneers). As they withdrew, the Confederates were able to advance closer to the line. The two left half guns then limbered up leaving one cannon isolated on the far left (near where you are standing). Private Thomas Aldrich, historian of the Rhode Island battery, described the scene:

> *Private William C. Barker was No. 4, and he stood holding the lanyard which was attached to the primer to fire the piece...Sergt. Amos M.C. Olney cried out: "Barker, why the d——l don't you fire that gun! pull! pull!"*[1]

The gun violently jolted backward as double-shotted canister spewed out into the charging North Carolinians; Fry's and Lowrance's regiments were ripped apart (see map 9). (Where these regiments crossed the fences along the Emmitsburg Road, one board, 14 inches wide and 16 feet long, showed 836 bullet holes.)[2]

Simultaneously, the 14th Connecticut, to the right of the Rhode Island gun, fired their muskets. Charles D. Page wrote of the account:

> ...[T]*he men dropped from the fence as if swept by a giant sickle swung by some powerful force of nature. Great gaps were formed in the line, the number of slain and wounded could not be estimated by numbers, but must be measured by yards. Yet on came the second line in full face of the awful carnage. No longer could the measured tread be heard, no longer were the orders of the commanding officers audible for the shrieks of the wounded and groans of the dying filled the air, but on they came, meeting with the same fate as their comrades. The third line wavered and faltered,*

> *even their courage forbidding them to face such a storm of musketry. The color-bearers now advanced, apparently in obedience to previous orders, and, attended by their color-guards, planted their battle flags in the ground much nearer. Then the firing being too hot for them, lay down, waiting for their men to advance and rally around them. One of them in particular was in advance of the others and planted his flag not more than ten rods* [55 yards] *from and in front of the center of the Fourteenth.*[3]

The 14th's commander, Major Theodore G. Ellis, asked for volunteers to capture the battleflag; several Connecticut soldiers jumped over the wall and ran toward the flag. Sergeant Major William B. Hincks swung his sword at the Confederates; he then seized the flag and sprinted back to the Cemetery Ridge line. The Confederates, overwhelmed and exhausted, retreated back to Seminary Ridge. Overall, the 14th Connecticut picked up the banners of the 1st Tennessee (Fry's brigade), the 16th North Carolina (Lowrance's brigade), and the 52d North Carolina (Marshall's brigade).[4]

One of the regiments opposing the 14th Connecticut was the 14th Tennessee. Captain June Kimble of this unit described his perspective:

> *...Soon shot and shell were plowing through the Confederate ranks; but on, steadily on the line moved without a waver or break save as gaps were rent by solid shot or exploding shell. The first fence was soon reached and quickly toppled over by hand and upon the points of bayonets. No check, but on we moved. The second fence shared the fate of the first, and without a halt the column went forward as if to victory. The third obstacle appeared, a strong, well-built post or slab fence, too strong to be quickly torn away. Realizing this, over the fence the Confederates sprang, thus pausing for a moment in some confusion; but re-forming quickly the line, still unbroken but terribly punished, rushed forward undismayed.*
>
> *....On it advanced until, having reached close range of the enemy's protected infantry, withering*

volleys of musketry, grape, double-charged canister, shot and shell shattered and mutilated as fine as body of Southern heroes as ever trod a battlefield...the remnant of those glorious Confederates kept going forward, until they silenced the guns and stood in the works of the enemy. Those of the enemy who remained in the works were prostrated at our feet, practically prisoners, with their arms upon the ground, not firing a shot.

For five, perhaps ten, minutes we held our ground and looked back for and prayed for support. It came not, and we knew that the battle of Gettysburg was ended.[5]

Go to Stop 7: Bryan's Farm

Stop 7

Bryan's Farm

"...they fell like wheat before the garner..."

—Captain George Bowen

While the Vermont regiments struck Kemper's right flank, Union troops to the far right hit the Confederate left flank.

Lieutenant Colonel Franklin Sawyer's 8th Ohio, deployed near the Emmitsburg Road, charged Colonel J. Brockenbrough. Many Confederates were killed or captured. The remaining men fell back to Seminary Ridge. With Brockenbrough's brigade gone, the 8th Ohio faced left. Near Bryan's farm, the 126th New York regiment, and two Napoleon cannon, swung left to join the 8th Ohio. The 1st Massachusetts Sharpshooters also joined in this group; infantrymen and cannon sent a deadly enfilading fire into the Confederate left flank. Davis's and Marshall's Confederate line disappeared; smoke engulfed the area and only small, unorganized clusters of soldiers continued the charge. Captain S.P. Wagg, of the 26th North Carolina, fell dead, shot through with shrapnel.[1] Lieutenant George Woodruff, commander of the two Union cannon, was hit through the body and mortally wounded.

Behind the wall the 12th New Jersey poured in musket fire from the front. Captain George Bowen, 12th New Jersey provided a description:

> *...we were armed with smoothbore muskets that shot one ball and buck, no good at long range but very effective at short. We waited until they were in the Emmitsburg road, a distance of not over 100 yards from us. Then we opened fire, pouring in the most deadly kind of fire, they fell like wheat before the garner, but still on they came until they were within a dozen feet of us when those that were left threw down their guns and surrendered. In passing a small house that stood on the opposite side*

> *of the Emmitsburg road, they broke into the movement known as "obstacle" breaking to the right and left, on passing this they filed back into line again as finely as if on dress parade. One man came up and got behind a small barn, not over 15 feet square that stood at the right of the Regt. I had just emptied my gun, he was pointing his gun right at me it seemed, Lieut. Acton was beside me shooting, I called his attention to him and said shoot him, he shot and the man fell, Acton said if he hit him it was in the head. Later I saw him with a bullet through the center of his forehead. During this fight, I fired 30 or 40 loads....*[2]

Members of the 12th New Jersey also noted a "smooth-cheeked lad,...the leader of thousands, [run]...forward through all that fire to fall dead...covered with wounds within twenty feet of [the Union] colors."[3]

One of these smooth-cheeked boys was Private Thomas F. McKie of the 11th Mississippi, "University Greys." He enlisted at 16 years of age in March of 1862. He fought in 13 engagements; nevertheless, Tommie, like all of the soldiers, yearned to go home. Several months before the battle of Gettysburg, Thomas wrote to his mother asking that she write President Jefferson Davis to get "him off." His mother, however, was unable to arrange this. On Friday afternoon, July 3, as he marched toward the Bryan farm, the young man was mortally wounded in the stomach and later died in a Union hospital.[4]

A fellow comrade, Lieutenant William Peel, 11th Mississippi, described their struggle:

> *...Four brave men had already fallen under the colors of our Reg't. & now the fifth bore them aloft, & rushed boldly forward, to embrace, if need be, the fate of the other four. The flag staff was now cut in two midway the flag, but without one moment's pause, the never-flinching little Irishman...his flag now dangling in graceless confusion, from one corner, still pushed fearlessly, upon the stone fence. Thirteen of our Reg't had concentrated upon the colors, as if to constitute ourselves its guard. We were some yards in advance of the line, & now*

> *found ourselves within about thirty yards of the stone fence. Immediately before us was a small framed house* [Bryan's barn]...*Springing forward, we secured its shelter, gaining at the same time, a position, within twenty five feet of the Yankees behind the fence.*[5]

Peel and his men found themselves in a precarious situation. They could either surrender or become a retreating target; the Mississippians surrendered. One Mississippi lieutenant fell within 10 feet of the Union line. (Some members of the 55th North Carolina also fought from behind the Bryan barn [see map 9].) Struck from the front and sides, and with continuous cannon fire from Cemetery Hill to Little Round Top, the Confederate tide ebbed (see map 10).[6]

Division commanders Pettigrew and Trimble had led closely behind their men, both receiving wounds. Pickett and his staff, however, supervised his division from the Codori farm. (Some historians believe he may have been near the Peach Orchard/Wentz house area.)[7] As Pickett rode back to Seminary Ridge, Lee stopped him and said, "General Pickett, place your division in [the] rear of this hill, and be ready to repel the advance of the enemy should they follow up their advantage."[8]

Pickett merely bowed his head and said, "General Lee, I have no division now. Armistead is down, Garnett is down, and Kemper is mortally wounded."[9] (Kemper survived.)

Lee answered, "Come, General Pickett, this has been my fight, and upon my shoulders rests the blame. The men and officers of your command have written the name of Virginia as high today as it has ever been written before."[10]

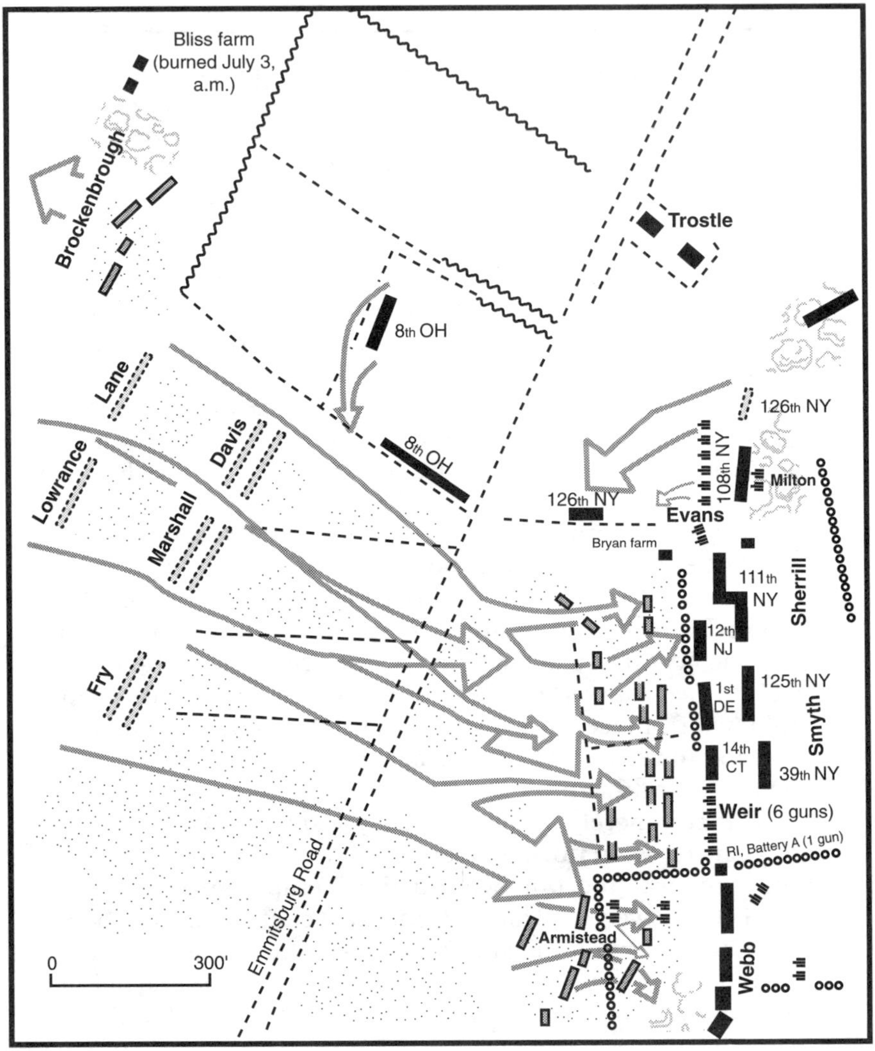

MAP 9

Stops 6 and 7: 1st Rhode Island, Battery A and Bryan's farm

Confederate left flank

As the Virginians break through the Union line Pettigrew's and Trimble's divisions advance toward the Union right. One Rhode Island gun and Lieutenant Gulian Weir's battery fire double-shotted canister into Fry's and Lowrance's brigades. Near the Bryan farm members of 11th Mississippi and 55th North Carolina attempt to hold their ground. The Confederate left flank, however, is hit by the 8th Ohio, 126th New York. Two Union cannon, commanded by Lieutenant John Egan, also swing left and fire into Pettigrew's and Trimble's left flank. The Confederate line disintegrates.

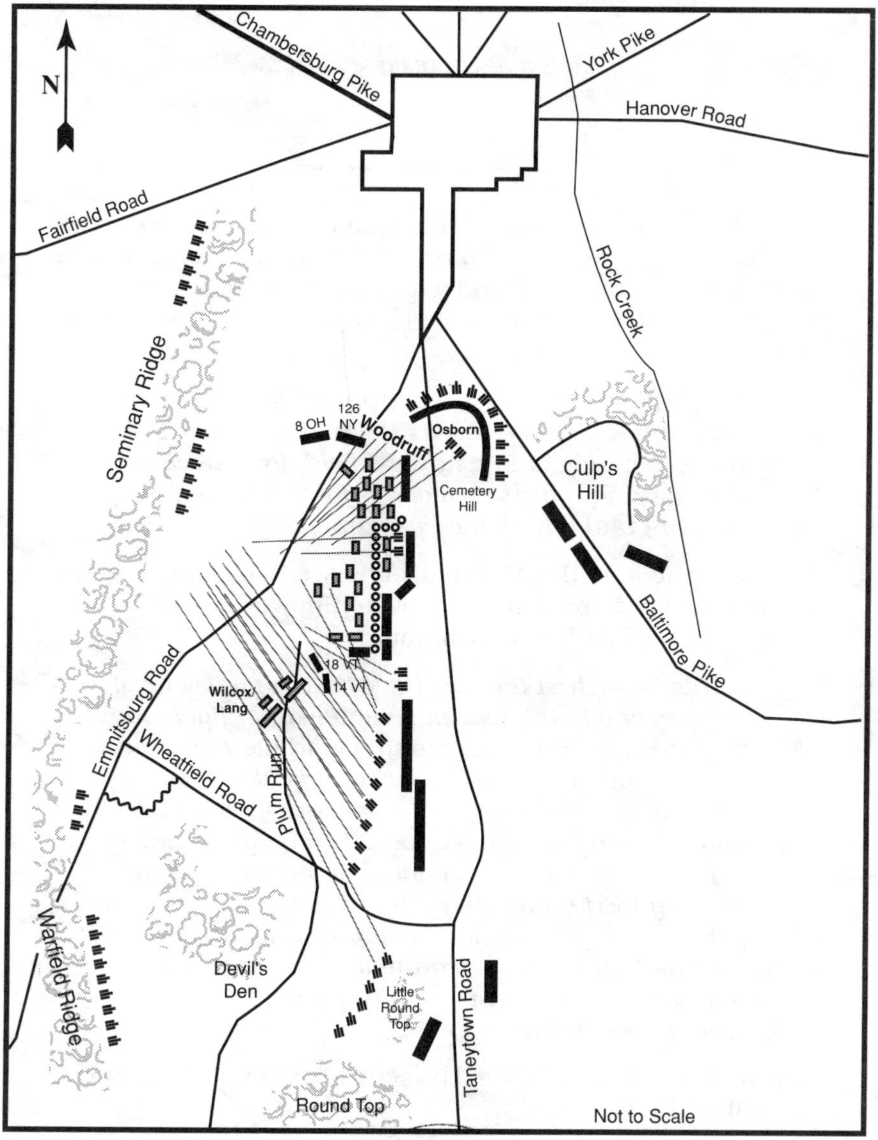

MAP 10

Stop 7: Bryan's farm

"Double-Envelope"

Pickett's, Pettigrew's, and Trimble's divisions are struck from the front and both flanks. Over 100 Union cannon from Cemetery Hill to Little Round Top continue to send a deadly crossfire into the Confederates. In two hours approximately 7,500 Southerners fall. Overall casualties from Seminary Ridge to Cemetery Ridge on July 2–3 are at least 10,185 Americans.

Aftermath

"...it is a heartbreaking sight..."

–Captain George Bowen

The actual infantry battle probably only lasted about half-an-hour to forty-five minutes. Yet, in that terrible time the carnage of the dead and wounded lay everywhere. Captain George Bowen, 12th New Jersey, vividly described the scene:

> *The field of battle is a sight never forgotten, the dead and wounded lay as thick as one ever saw sheaves of wheat in a harvest field, for a distance of a hundred yards or more in front and as far to the right and left as the eye can reach.*[1]

When night fell, the Union troops went out to give the wounded and dying water. The water, however, was bloody. Bowen continued his description:

> *...This is the first time we have had the privilege of going over a battlefield immediately after fight, one time is enough, the sight and sound were terrible, no one can give an idea of what it is like, the pain and misery of those poor fellows whom we shot down only a few hours ago—it is a heart breaking sight. Our men went through their haversacks taking any food they could find, they were well supplied as they have been living off the country. It sounds bad to rob a dead man, but we had nothing to eat, they had plenty for a living man, they were dead and would never want it any more.*[2]

The men of the 19th Massachusetts also recalled the horror of that night:

> *Ah! How sad were the hearts of the survivors that night! In front and to the left of the line were thousands of wounded men who were groaning and crying for help during the night. Those inside the*

> *line were cared for, but those lying between the lines were left to suffer, because neither side dared to go to their assistance.*[3]

An officer from the 126th New York stated the ground was "so thickly strewn with their dead that one could walk for rods on their dead bodies."[4]

Not only were hundreds of wounded and dead lying everywhere, but hundreds of dead horses lay in grotesque silence. Blood and entrails scattered the ground; the scene was sickening.

To make circumstances worse that night it began to rain. In Shakespearean fashion it washed the blood from the earth, but it also made life more unbearable for the wounded. It rained so heavily that some of the wounded, who lay in low areas, drowned. The two armies watched and cared for their wounded on July 4. That evening and the next day, the Confederate army began the long and arduous march back to Virginia; the Army of the Potomac followed. Thus, the battle of Gettysburg ended.

Summary of Friday, July 3

"...We gained nothing but glory..."

General Lee once again proposed a three-pronged attack. The main thrust was directed at the Union center; however, the Union army preempted the battle on the Confederate left flank. Due to lack of communication, or poor generalship, the Confederates decided to assault Culp's Hill without waiting for a simultaneous effort. The generals at the Confederate center were not ready to begin the charge until the afternoon. After five hours of fighting (6:30–11:30 a.m.) the Union troops compelled the Confederates to retreat from Culp's Hill.

At 1:00 p.m. the battle recommenced with a magnificent two-hour artillery duel. Then, around 3:00 p.m., 12,500 Confederates crossed a mile-wide field and charged the Union line on Cemetery Ridge. For an hour the battle raged, but the Confederates, exhausted and overwhelmed by numbers, were forced to retreat back to Seminary Ridge. One Virginia captain bluntly stated in a letter home, "We gained nothing but glory; and lost our bravest men."[1]

During the afternoon two cavalry battles took place. On the far Union right the Confederates were defeated. On the far Union left, their cavalry were repulsed by Confederate infantrymen.

Casualties: The Union army suffered 3,858 killed or wounded. The Confederates lost 6,326 killed or wounded. Overall 10,184 Americans fell on July 3, 1863.

A low estimate of casualties (including missing) from Seminary Ridge to Cemetery Ridge in two days of fighting is 10,185 (7,223 Confederates and 2,962 Union).

During the 24th reunion, 1887, members of the 69th Pennsylvania and Virginians from Pickett's division shake hands, epitomizing "Brothers again."

Pennsylvania at Gettysburg

This photograph shows the Copse of Trees from Armistead's and Garnett's view.

Pennsylvania at Gettysburg

Appendix I

Casualties on Cemetery Ridge

July 2–3

Confederate	Killed	Wounded	Missing
Perry's brigade (Lang), 742			
2d Fla.	24	71	11+
5th Fla.	39	77	23+
8th Fla.	17	80	11+
		Total Losses: 455, 61.3%	
Wright's brigade, 1,413			
3d Ga.	49	139	31
22d Ga.	41	70	60
48th Ga.	70	97	57
2d Ga. Batt.	24	37	21
		Total Losses: 696, 49.3%	
Pickett's division, 5,473			
		Total Losses: 2,904, 53.1%	
Kemper's brigade, 1,634			
1st Va.	27	73	13
3d Va.	30	41	57
7th Va.	31	82	36
11th Va.	34	86	26
24th Va.	47	83	33
		Total Losses: 699, 43.0%	
Armistead's brigade, 1,950			
9th Va.	24	70	83
14th Va.	14		
38th Va.	55	135	40
53d Va.	30		
57th Va.	32		
	Total Losses: approx. 1,223, 62.7%		
Garnett's brigade, 1,459			
8th Va.	39	79	60
18th Va.	54	134	57
19th Va.	42	41	68
28th Va.	44	65	73
56th Va.	51	72	66
		Total Losses: 945, 65.0%[1]	

Pettigrew's and Trimble's divisions experienced heavy casualties on the first day. The numbers below include the first-day casualties and the strength figure indicates the number within the division on the first day. The Confederates did not provide a casualty list for July 1.

	Killed	Wounded	Missing
Pettigrew's division, 7,458	779	1,935	644+
		Total Losses:	3,358, 45.0%
Trimble's division, 2,085			
Lane's brigade, 1,734	178	376	238
		Total Losses:	792, 45.7%
Scales' (Lowrance) brigade, 1,351	175	358	171
		Total Losses:	704, 52.1%

The 26th North Carolina went into the battle with 840 men. On the first day they fought against the 24th Michigan, Iron Brigade; they suffered heavy casualties. For the first and third day they counted 172 killed, 443 wounded, and 72 missing, 81.8%.

In just one hour, the entire Confederate loss for this charge was 7,500 men.[2]

The number of officers killed and wounded was extremely high: Garnett killed, Armistead mortally wounded, and Kemper severely wounded. Kemper never saw field duty again. Trimble, severely wounded in the leg, was captured. The Union surgeons were forced to amputate his leg. Pettigrew was slightly injured in the hand; he was mortally wounded two weeks later. Pickett, Davis, and Lane escaped unhurt.

Of their regimental officers only one survived unscathed, Major C.S. Peyton. Peyton, who had lost an arm in a previous battle, fought with the 19th Virginia (Garnett's brigade). Pickett's division had thirteen colonels; seven were killed, one mortally wounded, and the remaining wounded. Pettigrew's and Trimble's officers suffered as well. In Fry's (Archer's) brigade only two officers escaped injury; Marshall's (Pettigrew) brigade had all their officers killed or wounded except for one. Davis' brigade counted all their regimental officers killed or wounded.[3]

Two casualties of note were women. One Confederate woman was found dead on the field and another was wounded. She was taken to a Union field hospital where doctors amputated her leg. No names were revealed.[4]

July 2–3

Union	Killed	Wounded	Missing
1st Brigade, Second Division, II Corps			
Brigadier General William Harrow's brigade, 1,366			
19th Maine	29	170	4
15th Mass.	23	97	28
1st Minn. July 3d casualties only: 24 killed and wounded			
82 N.Y.	45	132	15
		Total Losses: 567, 56.2%	
2d Brigade, Second Division, II Corps			
Brigadier General Alexander Webb's brigade, 1,244			
69th Pa.	40	80	17
71st Pa.	21	58	19
72d Pa.	44	146	2
106th Pa.	9	54	1
		Total Losses: 491, 39.5%	
3d Brigade, Second Division, II Corps			
Colonel Norman J. Hall brigade, 922			
19th Mass.	9	61	7
20th Mass.	30	94	3
7th Mich.	21	44	0
42d N.Y.	15	55	4
59th N.Y.	6	28	0
		Total Losses: 377, 40.9%	
1st Massachusetts's Sharpshooters:	2	6	
2d Brigade, Third Division, II Corps			
Colonel Thomas Smyth's brigade, 1,069			
14th Conn.	10	52	4
1st Del.	10	54	13
12th N.J.	23	83	9
108th N.Y.	16	86	0
		Total Losses: 360, 33.8%	

3d Brigade, Third Division, II Corps

Colonel Eliakim Sherrill's brigade, 1,508

39th N.Y.	15	80	0
111th N.Y.	58	177	14
125th N.Y.	26	104	9
126th N.Y.	40	181	10

Total Losses: 714, 47.3%

8th Ohio: 18 killed, 83 wounded, and 1 missing

Union artillery, II Corps: 149 killed and wounded

3d Brigade, Third Division, I Corps

Brigadier General George Stannard's brigade, 1,950

13th Vt.	10	103	10
14th Vt.	19	67	21
16th Vt.	16	102	1

Total Losses: 349, 18.0%[5]

Like the Confederates, the Union general staff suffered heavily. Major General Winfield Hancock was severely wounded. Remarkably, Hancock survived the painful wound. Stannard was severely wounded, and a bullet pierced Gibbon's left shoulder. Eliakim Sherrill was shot through the stomach and killed. Thomas Smyth suffered a slight wound to his face; Alexander Webb was superficially injured. Doubleday, Hays, and Harrow were unharmed.

The Union regiment field officers also suffered great losses. After the battle, six were commanded by captains; a lieutenant led the 1st Delaware.[6]

Appendix II

"Captured" Confederate Flags

In the Civil War, capturing an enemy's flag represented great courage and strength. Color bearers and the color guard did not easily relinquish their flag. Following the assault the Union regiments counted their trophies and claimed them as "captured." How many flags were truly fought for and captured, however, we may never know. In some cases, while Union soldiers cared for the wounded, other infantrymen scoured the field in search of prizes, and they simply picked up the tattered flags from the mutilated bodies of the color guard. There was no struggle involved in this conquest.

Not including Brockenbrough's brigade, 38 regiments assaulted Cemetery Ridge. Each carried at least one flag. Of these units, Hancock's II Corps captured 28. In his official report, however, Hancock guessed about 33 colors were taken. Some Union soldiers hid them as personal trophies, and these were never reported. In addition to the II Corps' count, the 16th Vermont, of the I Corps, claimed two flags, one from the 8th Virginia and one from the 2d Florida. The number of Confederate flags lost was between 30 and 35.[1]

On one of the flags the Confederates wrote the following Latin inscription: *Dulce et Decorum Pro Mori Est Patria.* Translation: It is sweet and fitting to die for the fatherland (taken from Horace).[2]

Notes

INTRODUCTION

1. George R. Stewart, *Pickett's Charge: A Microhistory of the Final Attack at Gettysburg, July 3, 1863* (Dayton, Ohio: Morningside Bookshop, 1983), 80. *See also* William Frassanito, *Early Photography at Gettysburg* (Gettysburg: Thomas Publications, 1995), 181.
2. Frassanito, *Early Photography*, 232–34.
3. Ibid., 234.
4. Ibid., 180–81.
5. John W. Busey and David G. Martin, *Regimental Strengths and Losses at Gettysburg*. Hightstown, N.J.: Longstreet House, 1994. *See also* John M. Vanderslice, *Gettysburg Then and Now, The Field of American Valor Where and How the Regiments Fought and the Troops They Encountered* (New York: G.W. Dillingham Co., 1899), 120 and 132; *The War of the Rebellion: A Compilation of the Official Records of the Union and Confederate Armies*. Ser. I, Vol. XXVII, pt. 2 (Washington, D.C.: Government Printing Office, 1880–1901), 173. Hereafter cited as OR.
6. All information in this section is taken from OR, XXVII, pt. 2, 318–19.
7. Edwin B. Coddington, *The Gettysburg Campaign: A Study in Command* (New York: Charles Scribner's Sons, 1968), 337–38.
8. Albert A. Nofi, *Gettysburg Campaign: June and July 1863* (New York: W.H. Smith Publishers, 1986), 74.

STOP 1

1. OR, XXVII, pt. 2, 631–32. *See also* Harry W. Pfanz, *Gettysburg: The Second Day* (Chapel Hill, N.C.: University of North Carolina Press, 1987), 414.
2. George Gordon Meade, *The Battle of Gettysburg* (York, Pa: First Capitol Antiquarian Book and Paper Market, 1988), 89.
3. Ibid.
4. Stewart, *Pickett's Charge*, 115.
5. Coddington, *Gettysburg Campaign*, 494.
6. Ernest L. Waitt, *History of the Nineteenth Regiment Massachusetts Volunteer Infantry 1861–1865* (Salem, Mass.: The Salem Press, 1906), 237.
7. Ibid.
8. Richard Rollins, ed., *Pickett's Charge: Eyewitness Accounts* (Redondo Beach, Calif.: Rank and File Pub., 1994), 120.
9. Information about the number of guns disabled was taken from private conversation with Dave Shultz, authority on Union artillery at Gettysburg. *See also* George A. Bruce, *The Twentieth Regiment of Massachusetts Volunteer Infantry 1861–1865* (Boston, Mass.: Houghton, Mifflin and Company, 1906), 291.
10. Stewart, *Pickett's Charge*, 139.

11. *John Dooley: Confederate Soldier His War Journal*, edited by Joseph T. Durkin (Washington, D.C.: Georgetown University Press, 1945), 104.
12. David E. Johnston, *Four Years a Soldier* (Princeton: W.Va., 1887), 253.
13. Ibid., 271–72.
14. Lieutenant John H. Lewis, *Recollections from 1860 to 1865* (Washington, D.C.: Peake & Company, 1895), 84–85. *See also* Rollins, 97.
15. Rollins, *Pickett's Charge*, 104–5.
16. E.P. Alexander, *Fighting for the Confederacy: The Personal Recollections of General Edward Porter Alexander*, edited by Gary Gallagher (North Carolina: University of North Carolina Press, 1989), 258.
17. Ibid., 259.
18. Charles Hathaway, Licensed Battlefield Tour Guide, thinks the cannon Alexander saw were from the 1st Rhode Island Batteries A and B. Within these batteries, however, there were not 18 guns. It is most likely Alexander would not have had time to count the guns, and he may have just estimated 18.
19. Coddington, *Gettysburg Campaign*, 498.
20. Dave Shultz, *"Double Canister At Ten Yards:" The Federal Artillery And The Repulse of Pickett's Charge* (Redondo Beach, Calif.: Rank and File, 1995), 29.

STOP 2

1. Shultz, "*Double Canister A Ten Yards*," 29.
2. Stewart, *Pickett's Charge*, 173.
3. Ibid., 174.
4. Johnston, *Four Years*, 255.
5. David R. Riggs, *7th Virginia Infantry* (Lynchburg, Va.: H.E. Howard, Inc., 1985), 25.
6. Frank A. Haskell, *The Battle of Gettysburg* (Boston: Houghton, Mifflin and Company, 1958), 96.
7. Taken from Robert L. Brake's collection from Randolph A. Shotwell, 8th Regiment Virginia Volunteers. Virginia and North Carolina in the Battle of Gettysburg. "Southern Historical Monthly." pp. 112–13.
8. Stewart, *Pickett's Charge*, 187.
9. Dooley, *Confederate Soldier*, 106.
10. Ralph Orson Sturtevant, *Pictorial History of the Thirteenth Regiment Vermont Volunteers, War of 1861–1865* (Burlington, Vt.: The Free Press Association, 1910), 305.
11. Johnston, *Four Years*, 259.
12. Ibid.
13. Coddington, *Gettysburg Campaign*, 527–28.
14. Shultz, "Double Canister," 59.

STOP 3

1. Joseph Mayo, *Pickett's Charge at Gettysburg*, Southern Historical Society Papers, Vol. 34, edited by R.A. Brock (Richmond, Va.: Published by the Society, 1906), 332.
2. Undated remarks by Andrew Cowan. 1st Independent Battery Artillery, Andrew Cowan. Box 10: Federal Units, Minnesota-New York. Robert Blake Collection. United States Military History Institute, Archives Division. *See also*, Coddington, *Gettysburg Campaign*, 516.

3. Champ Clark, *Gettysburg: The Confederate High Tide* (Alexandria, Va: Time Life Book Series, 1985), 141.

STOP 4

1. OR, Vol. 27, Ser. I , Pt. 2, 386.
2. D. Scott Hartwig. "It Struck Horror To Us All," *Gettysburg Magazine*, January 1991, no. 4, 98.
3. Anthony W. McDermott, *A Brief History of the 69th Regiment Pennsylvania Veteran Volunteers* (Philadelphia, Pa: D.J. Gallagher & Co., 1887), 32.
4. Ida Lee Johnston, "Over the Stone Wall at Gettysburg," *Confederate Veteran*, Vol. 31, 249.
5. Clark, *Gettysburg*, 141.
6. J.F. Crocker, *My Capture at Gettysburg and prison reminiscences* (Suffolk, Va.: Robert Hardy Pubs, 1986), 37–44.
7. Lieutenant J. Irving Sale, *The Philadelphia Press*, 4 July 1887, p. 1, col. 1. Citation found in Robert Brake's Collection, the New York 1st Independent Battery, Artillery, folder, in Archives, U.S. Military History Institute, Carlisle, Pa.
8. Stewart, *Pickett's Charge*, 260.
9. Wayne E. Motts, *"Trust In God And Fear Nothing," General Lewis Armistead, CSA* (Gettysburg: Farnsworth House Military Impression, 1994), 49.

STOP 5

1. Haskell, *Battle of Gettysburg*, 104; *see also* Coddington, *Gettysburg Campaign*, 518.
2. *History of the Nineteenth Regiment: Massachusetts Volunteer Infantry, 1861–1865* (Salem: Salem Press Co., 1906), 242.
3. *Reunions of the Nineteenth Maine Regiment Association, Portland, Bath, Belfast, Augusta, and Richmond* (Augusta, Maine: Sprague, Owen & Nash, 1878), 12–13.

STOP 6

1. Thomas M. Aldrich, *The History of Battery A, First Rhode Island Light Artillery in the War to Preserve the Union 1861–1865* (Providence, R.I.: Snow and Farnham, 1904), 216.
2. Stewart, *Pickett's Charge*, 260.
3. Charles D. Page, *History of the Fourteenth Regiment, Connecticut Volunteer Infantry* (Meriden, Conn.: Horton Printing Co., 1906), 152.
4. *See* Page, 154–56 and 161. *See also* Bruce A. Trinque, "Arnold's Battery and the 26th North Carolina," *Gettysburg Magazine*. January, 1995 no. 12, 63.
5. Rollins, *Pickett's Charge*, 268–69.

STOP 7

1. Walter Clark, ed. *Histories of the Several Regiments and Battalions from North Carolina in the Great War 1861–65*, Vol. II (Goldsboro, N.C.: Nash Brothers, Book and Job Printers, 1901), 356–58.
2. Rollins, *Pickett's Charge*, 288–89.
3. Samuel Toombs, *New Jersey Troops in the Gettysburg Campaign from June 5 to July 31, 1863* (New Jersey: Longstreet House, 1988), 300.

4. Maud Morrow Brown, *The University Greys, Company A Eleventh Mississippi Regiment Army of Northern Virginia 1862–1865* (Richmond, Va.: Garrett and Massie Inc., 1940), 46.
5. Rollins, *Pickett's Charge*, 275.
6. Franklin Sawyer. *A Military History of the 8th Regiment Ohio Volunteer Infantry: Its Battles, Marches and Army Movements*. George A. Groot, ed. (Cleveland: Fairbanks and Co., 1881), 131–32.
7. Kathleen R. Georg and John W. Busey. *Nothing But Glory: Pickett's Division at Gettysburg* (Hightstown, N.J.: Longstreet House, 1987), 202.
8. This conversation can be found in Stewart, *Pickett's Charge*, 256–57.
9. Ibid.
10. Ibid.

AFTERMATH

1. George Bowen, *The Valley Forge Journal*, 132.
2. Ibid., 134–35.
3. Waitt, *History of the Nineteenth Regiment*, 245.
4. Stewart, *Pickett's Charge*, 260.

SUMMARY

1. Stewart, *Pickett's Charge*, 266.

APPENDIX I

1. John W. Busey and David G. Martin, *Regimental Strengths and Losses at Gettysburg*. Hightstown, N.J.: Longstreet House, 1994.
2. Ibid., 266.
3. Stewart, *Pickett's Charge*, 268–69.
4. *See* note 105 in Gregory A. Coco, ed., *On the Bloodstained Field: 130 Human Interest Stories of the Campaign and Battle of Gettysburg* (Gettysburg: Thomas Publications, 1987), 55.
5. Numbers found in Busey and Martin, *Regimental Strengths and Losses at Gettysburg*.
6. For Hancock's wound *see* Stewart, *Pickett's Charge*, 233; Gibbon's injury *see* Stewart, 224. For Union regimental losses in officers see Stewart, 268.

APPENDIX II

1. Stewart, *Pickett's Charge*, 269.
2. Richard Rollins, personal conversation, February 1997.

Bibliography

Alexander, Edward Porter. *Fighting for the Confederacy: The Personal Recollections of General Edward Porter Alexander.* Editor Gary Gallagher. North Carolina: University of North Carolina Press, 1989.

Aldrich, Thomas M. *The History of Battery A, First Rhode Island Light Artillery in the War to Preserve the Union 1861–1865.* Providence, R.I.: Snow and Farnham, 1904.

Arnold-Friend, Louise. *Gettysburg Campaign and Battle, June–July, 1863: A Working Bibliography.* Carlisle, Pa.: U.S. Army Military History Institute, 1993.

Banes, Charles H. *History of the Philadelphia Brigade.* Philadelphia: J.B. Lippincott & Co., 1876.

Bell, Robert T. *11th Virginia Infantry.* Lynchburg, Va.: H.E. Howard, Inc., 1985.

Brake, Robert L. Collection, Archives, U.S. Army Military History Institute; Walter F. Beyer and O.F. Keydel, *Deeds of Valor*; Ida Lee Johnston "Over the Stone Wall at Gettysburg," *Confederate Veteran*, Vol. XXXI, p. 249.

Brown, Maud Morrow. *The University Greys: Company A Eleventh Mississippi Regiment Army of Northern Virginia, 1861–1865.* Richmond, Va.: Garrett and Massie, Inc., 1940.

Bruce, George A., Brevet Lieutenant Colonel. *The Twentieth Regiment of Massachusetts Volunteer Infantry 1861–1865.* Boston, Mass.: Houghton, Mifflin and Company, 1906.

Busey, John W. and David G. Martin. *Regimental Strengths and Losses at Gettysburg.* Hightstown, N.J.: Longstreet House, 1994.

Campbell, Eric. "'Remember Harper's Ferry': The Degradation, Humiliation, and Redemption of Col. George L. Willard's Brigade, Part 2." *Gettysburg Magazine.* 8 (Jan. 1993): pp. 95–111.

Carpenter, Alfred P., Co. K, First Minnesota Volunteers Infantry. "Letter on the Battle of Gettysburg, Warrenton Junction, Va., 30 July, 1863. Minnesota Historical Society: From Robert Brake Collection, U.S. Army Military History Institute, Carlisle, Pa.

Clark, Champ. *Gettysburg: The Confederate High Tide.* Alexandria, Va.: Time Life Book Series, 1985.

Clark, Walter, ed. *Histories of the Several Regiments and Battalions from North Carolina in the Great War 1861–65.* 5 Vols. Goldsboro, N.C.: Nash Brothers, Book and Job Printers, 1901.

Coco, Gregory A., ed. *On the Bloodstained Field: 130 Human Interest Stories of the Campaign and Battle of Gettysburg.* Gettysburg: Thomas Publications, 1987.

———, ed. *On the Bloodstained Field II: 132 More Human Interest Stories of the Campaign and Battle of Gettysburg.* Gettysburg: Thomas Publications, 1989.

Coddington, Edwin B. *The Gettysburg Campaign: A Study in Command.* New York: Charles Scribner's Sons, 1968.

Colvill, William Jr., Colonel First Minnesota. "Account of Colonel Colvill at the Battle of Gettysburg." Letter to the Editor, *The Minneapolis Daily Tribune,* 28 July, 1884. From the Robert L. Brake Collection, U.S. Army Military History Institute, Carlisle, Pa.

Cowan, Andrew, Capt. of the 1st New York Battery. Undated remarks by Andrew Cowan...in response to Alexander Stewart Webb...on a sketch of the repulse of Pickett's Charge. Alexander Stewart Webb Collection, Yale University Library. U.S. Army Military History Institute, Carlisle, Pa.

Crocker, J.F. *My Capture at Gettysburg and prison reminiscences.* Suffolk, Va.: Robert Hardy Pubs., 1986.

Divine, John E., ed. *8th Virginia Infantry.* Lynchburg, Va.: H.E. Howard, Inc., 1983. U.S. Army Military History Institute, Carlisle, Pa.

Dooley, John Edward. *John Dooley: Confederate Soldier His War Journal.* Editor, Joseph T. Durkin. Washington, D.C.: Georgetown University Press, 1945.

Dowdey, Clifford. *Death of a Nation: The Story of Lee and His Men at Gettysburg*. New York: Alfred A. Knopf, 1958.

Downey, Fairfax. *The Guns at Gettysburg*. New York: David McKay Company Inc., 1958.

Frassanito, William. *Early Photography at Gettysburg*. Gettysburg: Thomas Publications, 1995.

Gunn, Ralph White. *24th Virginia Infantry*. Lynchburg, Va.: H.E. Howard Inc., 1987.

Hadden, R. Lee. "The Granite Glory: The 19th Maine at Gettysburg." *Gettysburg Magazine*. 13 (July 1995): pp. 50–64.

Harrison-Georg, Kathleen R. and John W. Busey. *Nothing But Glory: Pickett's Division at Gettysburg*. Editor David G. Martin. Hightstown, N.J.: Longstreet House, 1987.

———. *The Location of the Monuments, Markers, and Tablets on Gettysburg Battlefield*. Gettysburg: Thomas Publications, 1993.

Hartwig, D. Scott. "It Struck Horror To Us All." *Gettysburg Magazine*. 4 (Jan. 1991): pp. 89–101.

Haskell, Frank A. *The Battle of Gettysburg*. Boston: Houghton, Mifflin and Company, 1958.

Holcombe, Return I. *History of the First Regiment Minnesota Volunteer Infantry: 1861–1864*. Minnesota: Easto and Masterman, 1916.

Hoke, Jacob. *The Great Invasion of 1863 or General Lee in Pennsylvania*. Ohio: W.J. Shuey Publisher, 1887.

Johnston, David E. *Four Years a Soldier*. Princeton, W.Va.: 1887.

Lash, Gary G. "The Philadelphia Brigade at Gettysburg." *Gettysburg Magazine*. 7 (July 1992): pp. 97–114.

Lewis, John H. *Recollections from 1860 to 1865*. Washington, D.C.: Peake & Company, 1895.

Livermore, William Roscoe. *The Story of the Civil War: A Concise Account of the War in the United States of America Between 1861 and 1865, in the Continuation of the Story by John Codman Ropes*. Part III: The Campaigns of 1863 to July 10. Book II: Vicksburg, Port Hudson, Tullahoma, and Gettysburg. New York: G.P. Putnam's Sons, [1894] 1913.

Loehr, Charles T. *War History of the Old First Virginia Infantry Regiment, Army of Northern Virginia.* Richmond, Va.: WM. Ellis Jones, 1884.

———. *The 'Old First' Virginia at Gettysburg.* Southern Historical Society Papers. Vol. 22. Richmond, Va.: Published by the Society, 1904.

Long, Roger. "Over the Wall." *Gettysburg Magazine.* 13 (July 1995): pp. 64–75.

Longstreet, James. "Lee's Invasion of Pennsylvania." In *Battles and Leaders of the Civil War.* Vol. III. Edited by Robert U. Johnson and Clarence C. Buel. New York: Castle, 1888.

———. *From Manassas to Appomattox: Memoirs of the Civil War in America.* New York: Mallard Press, 1991.

McDermott, Anthony W. *A Brief History of the 69th Regiment Pennsylvania Veteran Volunteers.* Philadelphia, Pa.: D.J. Gallagher & Co., 1887.

Magner, Blake A. and Steven J. Wright. "John Gibbon: The Man and the Monument." *Gettysburg Magazine.* 13 (July 1995).

Maine at Gettysburg: Report of the Maine Commissioners. Portland, Maine: Lakeside, 1898.

Mayo, Joseph. *Pickett's Charge at Gettysburg.* Southern Historical Society Papers. Vol. 34. Editor R.A. Brock. Richmond, Va.: Published by the Society, 1906.

Meade, George Gordon. *The Battle of Gettysburg.* York, Pa.: First Capitol Antiquarian Book and Paper Market, 1988.

Michigan at Gettysburg. Detroit: Winn and Hammond, 1889.

Motts, Wayne E. *"Trust In God And Fear Nothing," General Lewis Armistead, CSA.* Gettysburg: Farnsworth House Military Impression, 1994.

New York Monuments Commission for the Battlefields of Gettysburg and Chattanooga. *Final Report on the Battlefield of Gettysburg.* 3 Vols. Albany, N.Y.: J.B. Lyon Company, Printers, 1900.

Nicholson, John P., ed. *Pennsylvania at Gettysburg: Ceremonies at the Dedication of the Monuments Erected by the Commonwealth of Pennsylvania.* 3 vols. Harrisburg, Pa.: Wm. Stanley Ray, State Printer, 1904.

Niven, John. *Connecticut for the Union: The Role of the State in the Civil War.* New Haven, Conn.: Yale University Press, 1965.

Nofi, Albert A. *Gettysburg Campaign: June and July 1863.* New York: W. H. Publishers, 1986.

O'Brien, Kevin E. "To Unflinchingly Face Danger and Death:" *Gettysburg Magazine.* 12 (Jan. 1995): pp. 7–24.

Osborn, Maj. Thomas Ward. *The Eleventh Corps Artillery at Gettysburg. The Papers of Major Thomas Ward Osborn Chief of Artillery.* Editor Herb S. Crumb. Hamilton, N.Y.: Edmonston Publishing, Inc., 1991.

Page, Charles D. *History of the Fourteenth Regiment, Connecticut Volunteer Infantry.* Meriden, Conn.: Horton Printing Co., 1906.

Palmer, Edwin Frederick. *The Second Brigade or, Camp Life.* Montelier: E.P. Walton, 1864.

Pfanz, Harry W. *Gettysburg: The Second Day.* Chapel Hill, N.C.: University of North Carolina Press, 1987.

Philadelphia Press. 3 July, 1887, pg. 2, col. 4. From Brake Collection, U.S. Army Military History Institute, Carlisle, Pa.

———. 4 July, 1887, pg. 1, col. 6. From Brake Collection, U.S. Army Military History Institute, Carlisle, Pa.

Plummer, John W. Sergeant Co. D, First Minnesota Volunteer Infantry, "Letter to His Brother," *State Atlas*, Minneapolis, 26 August 1863: From the Brake Collection, U.S. Army Military History Institute, Carlisle, Pa.

Reeve, E.P. *Casualties in the Old First at Gettysburg.* Southern Historical Society Papers. Vol. 27. Richmond, Va.: Published by the Society, 1889.

Reunions of the Nineteenth Maine Regiment Association, Portland, Bath, Belfast, Augusta, and Richmond. Augusta, Maine: Sprague, Owen & Nash, 1878.

Riggs, David F. *7th Virginia Infantry.* Lynchburg, Va.: H.E. Howard Inc., 1985.

Rollins, Richard. *Pickett's Charge: Eyewitness Accounts.* Redondo Beach, Calif.: Rank and File Pub., 1994.

Saint Paul's Daily Press, 25 July, 1863, pg. 1. From Brake Collection, U.S. Army Military History Institute, Carlisle, Pa.

Sale, Lt. J. Irving. *The Philadelphia Press*, 4 July, 1887, pg. 1, col. 1. Citation found in Robert Brake's Collection, the New York 1st Independent Battery, Artillery, in Archives, U.S. Military History Institute, Carlisle, Pa.

Sawyer, Franklin. *A Military History of the 8th Regiment Ohio Volunteer Infantry: Its Battles, Marches and Army Movements*. Editor, George A. Groot. Cleveland: Fairbanks & Co., 1881. U.S. Military History Institute, Carlisle, Pa.

Shotwell, Randolph A. Virginia and North Carolina in the Battle of Gettysburg. *Southern Historical Monthly*. Brake Collection, see 8th Virginia. U.S. Military History Institute, Carlisle, Pa.

Shultz, David. *"Double Canister At Ten Yards:" The Federal Artillery And the Repulse of Pickett's Charge*. Redondo Beach, Calif.: Rank and File, 1995.

Stackpole, Edward J. *They Met at Gettysburg*. Harrisburg, Pa.: The Stackpole Company, 1956.

Stanchak, John E., ed. "Gettysburg: The Full Story of the Struggle," *The Civil War Times*. Harrisburg, Pa.: Historical Times Inc., 1988.

Stewart, George R. *Pickett's Charge: A Microhistory of the Final Attack at Gettysburg, July 3, 1863*. Dayton, Ohio: Morningside Bookshop, 1983.

Sturtevant, Ralph Orson. *Pictorial History of the Thirteenth Regiment Vermont Volunteers, War of 1861–1865*. Burlington, Vt.: The Free Press Association, 1910.

Taylor, Michael W. "North Carolina in the Pickett-Pettigrew-Trimble Charge at Gettysburg."*Gettysburg Magazine*. 8 (Jan. 1993): pp. 67–95.

Toombs, Samuel. *New Jersey Troops in the Gettysburg Campaign from June 5 to July 31, 1863*. Reprint No. 202. New Jersey: Longstreet House, 1988. U.S. Army Military History Institute, Carlisle, Pa.

Trinque, Bruce A. "Arnold's Battery and the 26th North Carolina." *Gettysburg Magazine*. 12 (Jan. 1995): pp. 61–68.

Vanderslice, John M. *Gettysburg: Then and Now: The Field of American Valor Where and How the Regiments Fought and the Troops They Encountered.* New York: G.W. Dillingham Co., 1899.

Waitt, Ernest L. *History of the Nineteenth Regiment Massachusetts Volunteer Infantry 1861–1865.* Salem, Mass.: The Salem Press, 1906.

Wallace, Lee A., Jr. *1st Virginia Infantry.* Lynchburg, Va.: H.E. Howard, Inc., 1984.

———. *3rd Virginia Infantry.* Lynchburg, Va.: H.E. Howard, Inc., 1986.

The War of the Rebellion: A Compilation of the Official Records of the Union and Confederate Armies. Ser. I, Vol. XXVII, pts. 1, 2, 3. Washington, D.C.: Government Printing Office, 1880–1901.

Young, Jesse Bowman. *The Battle of Gettysburg.* Dayton, Ohio: Morningside Bookshop, 1976.

Index

Photograph page numbers in italics.